THE CORK BLACKROCK & PASSAGE RAILWAY

by
Stanley C. Jenkins, BA, PGCE, MA
(Incorporating material by A.T. Newham)

STATIO BENE FIDE CARINIS

D1354610

THE OAKWOOD PRESS

© S.C. Jenkins & Oakwood Press 1993

ISBN 0 85361 405 9

First Edition 1970
Second Enlarged Edition 1993

Typeset by Gem Publishing Company, Brightwell, Wallingford, Oxfordshire.
Printed by Alpha Print (Oxon) Ltd, Witney, Oxfordshire.

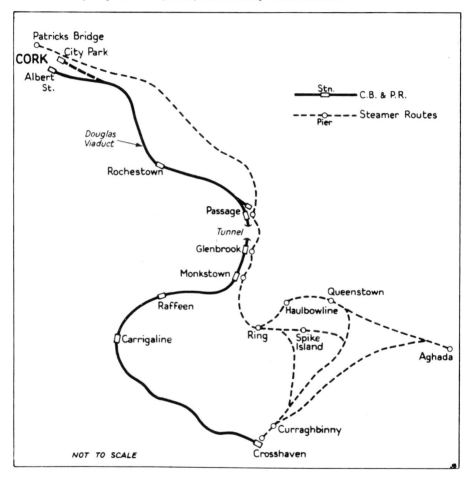

Published by
The OAKWOOD PRESS
P.O.Box 122, Headington, Oxford.

Contents

Introduction

The Cork Blackrock & Passage Railway was unusual in a number of ways. It was opened in 1850 as a short, 5 ft 3 in. gauge suburban line, but after 50 years of successful operation it was extended to Crosshaven and converted to the 3 ft gauge. Several years previously (1881) the CB&PR Directors had secured statutory powers to operate steamers on the River Lee in connection with the trains at Passage, and serving the coastal resorts of Queenstown, Glenbrook, Monkstown, Crosshaven, and Aghada, together with (on occasions) the nearby Royal Naval dockyard at Haulbowline. These vessels competed with those of older-established operators, and their high operating costs led to a decision, in 1894, to extend the railway, as already mentioned, to Crosshaven.

In narrow gauge days the system had two unusual features for such a line – a double track section between Cork and Blackrock, and a tunnel from Passage to the next station at Glenbrook. Like other Irish lines, the CB&PR suffered severely during the political troubles of 1920–23, and in 1925 the local company became part of the Great Southern Railways. By that time, the growth of rival forms of transport had rendered the line totally uneconomic, and it was closed to all traffic in 1932.

The CB&PR was an obscure line that received little publicity, and the publication of a short history of the route in 1970 filled a useful gap in the story of the Irish narrow gauge. The original book has been out of print for several years and sadly, the author – Mr A.T. Newham – has since died. When the opportunity arose to produce a new history of the CB&PR, I was asked to upgrade and expand the earlier narrative. I initially tried to keep as much as possible of Mr Newham's original work, but in the event numerous points were expanded, amended or clarified (for example the matter of locomotive bells). The old text has been used as basis for Chapters 1, 2 and 5 of the present work, and an expanded 'route' section has been added and this is largely my own work. Similarly, Mr Newham had, perhaps tactfully, omitted to mention the Potato Famine of 1845–49, the Black & Tan campaign, or the Anglo-Irish treaty of 1921 and insofar as these events impinged upon the railway I have included some additional data in the hope that this vital background information will enhance the purely 'railway' sections (it seemed important, for instance, to tell readers that 26 Irish counties became detached from the United Kingdom in 1921). It follows that any opinions or prejudices that may be detected are entirely my own, and not Mr Newham's.

Stanley C. Jenkins,
Witney, Oxfordshire
1993

Historical Summary

Company of Origin
Cork Blackrock & Passage Railway, incorporated by Act of 16th July, 1846 to construct a line from Cork to Passage West, a distance of 6 miles 49 chains. Capital of £130,000 with £43,330 in loans. By Act of 25th July, 1847 the company was empowered to build an extension of 1 mile 30 chains to Monkstown, but these powers were allowed to lapse.

A further Act of 7th August, 1896 permitted an extension to Crosshaven, with a new issue of £110,000 in shares and £35,000 by loan.

Dates of Opening
Cork (City Park) to Passage .... 8th June, 1850
Cork (Albert Street) to Marina .... 6th February, 1873
Passage to Monkstown .... 1st August, 1902
Monkstown to Carrigaline .... 15th June, 1903
Carrigaline to Crosshaven .... 1st June, 1904

Dates of Closure
Cork City Park to Marina (superseded) .... 6th February, 1873
Crosshaven to Monkstown .... 31st May, 1932
Monkstown to Cork Albert Street .... 10th September, 1932

Gauge of Line
Originally 5 ft 3 in., but converted to 3 ft narrow gauge between Cork and Passage on 29th October, 1900; the remainder of the line to Crosshaven was narrow gauge from its inception.

Some Relevant Acts of Parliament
16th July, 1846 – Incorporation of CB & PR company
25th July, 1847 – Further powers and extension of line
13th May, 1872 – Amendments to Cork Improvements Act
7th August, 1896 – CB & PR Extension Act
9th August, 1901 – Additional capital, etc.

Length of Line
Original line from Cork (City Park) to Passage (Old Station) .... 6¼ miles
Extension from Passage to Crosshaven .... 9¼ miles
Total distance (Cork Albert Street to Crosshaven) .... 15¾ miles

Mode of Operation (1906)
Double line block from Cork to Blackrock, and Webb-Thompson train staff on remaining (single line) sections. The passing stations were Rochestown, Monkstown, Carrigaline and Crosshaven, with an additional crossing loop to the west of the platform at Passage.

5

PATRICK'S BRIDGE. CORK. 2671. W.L.

The CB&PR goods vessel SS *Rostellan* discharges her cargo at St Patrick's Bridge, Cork. This screw-powered steamer could also carry passengers, although her low bulwarks and lack of seating (or other amenities) suggest that she would only have been pressed into passenger services in real emergencies!

National Library of Ireland

Chapter One

Construction, Opening and Early Years (1845–1867)

Situated in the southernmost part of Ireland, the City of Cork was, in the early 19th century, a relatively prosperous port. The nearby village of Cove (which, in later years, as Queenstown, would become famous as a port of call for transatlantic liners) was merely a fishing settlement, but it had already started to develop as a much favoured resort, direct access from Cork being provided by paddle steamers on the River Lee. Operated by 'the City of Cork Proprietors', these vessels sailed to and from St Patrick's Bridge, the 12 mile journey to Cove being accomplished in about 1½ hours. By 1836, five steamers were in operation, and thousands of people were being carried each year; the fares from Cork were 9d. for cabin passengers and 6d. for ordinary deck travellers.

There was clearly a market for improved travel facilities between Cork and newly-fashionable resorts such as Cove, and it is hardly surprising that, in the 1830s, proposals were made for a 6½ mile railway between Cork and Passage West. Passage, which stood on the narrow west passage between the inner harbour (Lough Mahon) and the estuary of the River Lee, was then an important ship building centre, with ferry connections to nearby Cove. There were, moreover, suggestions that Passage could be developed as a major transatlantic port, and in these circumstances there was a pressing need for direct rail access to and from the City of Cork.

Early Railway Development

Railways came to Ireland at a surprisingly early date, the first proposals being put forward in the 1820s when ambitious entrepreneurs had sought Parliamentary consent for a system of lines linking Belfast and Dublin. Sadly, this early scheme failed to gain Parliamentary approval, but tangible progress was made in the following decade, the first railway to open in Ireland being the pioneering Dublin & Kingstown line in 1834. The remarkable success of the Dublin & Kingstown must have encouraged the promoters of the Cork project to persist with their own scheme, and an Act was successfully obtained in 1837, with powers to raise capital of £266,000 for construction of the 'Cork & Passage Railway'. Sadly, preliminary difficulties were so great that the scheme was abandoned at an early stage.

Eight years later, at the height of the Railway Mania, powers were sought for three similar railways: the Cork Passage & Kinsale Railway, the Cork & Passage Railway, and the Cork Blackrock Passage & Monkstown Railway.

These nebulous schemes eventually resulted in an Act of incorporation for the Cork Blackrock & Passage Railway (9 & 10 Vic. cap. 148). The Act, passed on 16th July, 1846, empowered the promoters to construct a railway commencing in Cork and terminating on the steam packet quay at Passage. The line, to be built on the Irish broad gauge of 5 ft 3 in., would be 6 miles 49 chains in length, and capital of £130,000 with loans of £43,000 was authorised to pay for its construction.

The first meeting of the newly-incorporated CB & PR Company was held in Cork shortly after the passing of the Act, and at that meeting the assembled shareholders were told that the first call on shares had been paid up in full, while the second was 'paid up with the exception of about 100 shares'. The Directors assured them that they had 'many advantages before them'. There was not a single engineering difficulty upon the whole line, and it was confidently expected that the railway 'would be open early in 1848'.

The Secretary then read a Directors' report, and an account of receipts and expenditure up to 1st November, 1846. From the accounts, it appeared that a balance of £5,508 remained in hand after paying off all the liabilities that had been incurred, that balance being 'independent of the call in course of payment'.

The Directors were confident that work would commence before 1st March, 1847, and it was predicted that the line 'would be open to the public by 1st June, 1848'. It was pointed out that, if various deviations were made in the authorised route, the company would be able to save 'several thousand pounds'. This change would make it necessary to 'run from Horsehead to the Steam Packet Wharf at Passage, along the strand in front of Toureen Terrace' in order to obtain the best and most practicable alignments for any future extensions to Monkstown or beyond; this would necessitate a further Act of Parliament, 'in which the extension to Monkstown could be obtained at a trifling additional cost'.

The reports were adopted, and after further business had been conducted, the Chairman concluded the meeting on a note of optimism. His remarks were reported as follows in a contemporary newspaper:

> Doctor Lyons, in the course of some observations, said that the company had actually in hand £9,500, and when the last call fell due, which would be in about a fortnight, they would have £11,500 . . . this would not be sufficient to warrant the Directors in entering into a contract for the line, but by 1st March they would contrive to have £25,000 in hand, and would then have no hesitation in pledging themselves to a respectable contractor for £40,000 or £50,000.
>
> Two or three respectable men had offered to execute the earthworks and bridges within £50,000, and have them completed in nine months, and lay down the sleepers and rails in three months more – thereby opening the line in January 1848. It was now, however, intended to get a new Act, so as to lower the line three or four feet.
>
> After the election of Directors, and a . . . conversation on the prospects of the company, a resolution authorising the Directors to proceed to Parliament for an amended Act was passed, and the meeting adjourned.

The Cork Blackrock & Passage scheme was, at this early stage, progressing satisfactorily, and with talk of a public opening in the early part of 1848, most of the CB & PR proprietors were confident that their project could be brought to a successful conclusion.

Unfortunately, bad harvests at the end of 1845 had sparked off a major economic crisis – particularly in southern and western Ireland where the population had been entirely dependent on the potato crop. The City of Cork was soon thronged with thousands of starving paupers, the disaster being compounded by an outbreak of fever. In March 1847 the entire city was placed in quarantine – over 750 people having died in the local workhouse in that month alone.

The supporters of the Cork Blackrock & Passage scheme were, in the meantime, busily raising capital. Although the failed harvests of the mid to late 1840s were a major disaster for Ireland (and even for parts of England and Scotland), the CB&PR promoters were not unduly concerned; being major landowners, or successful professional men, they were not personally touched by 'The Great Hunger' – indeed, the relatively prosperous areas to the east of Cork seem to have escaped the worst effects of the famine.

On 25th July, 1847 a further Act of Parliament (10 & 11 Vic. cap. 49) provided consent for a 1 mile 37 chain extension from Passage to Monkstown Baths. This same Act also allowed the company to make certain deviations of the route between Cork and Passage, while at the same time the authorised capital of the Cork Blackrock & Passage Railway was increased to £170,000 (in £20 shares) with an additional £56,663 in loans. The total capital – if fully subscribed – would thus be no less than £226,663 for a railway which, if completed throughout, would be little more than 8 miles long.

Construction Begins

Undeterred by the worsening social and economic crisis, the promoters pressed on with their scheme, and construction of the 8 mile 6 chain railway commenced in the summer of 1847. A contract for building the line was awarded to Messrs Moore of Dublin, the Engineer being the well-known Sir John Macneill (1793–1880). One of Ireland's greatest engineers, Sir John was involved with numerous other lines – notably the Great Southern & Western Railway which, by 1847, was still under construction for much of its length between Dublin and Cork.

The first sod of the Cork Blackrock & Passage Railway was cut at a site near Dundanion Castle, some two miles from Cork, on Tuesday 15th June, 1847. The ceremonial cutting of the first turf was performed by Lady Deane, and those present at this auspicious occasion included the CB&PR Directors, the contractor, and the Mayor of Cork, Andrew Roche.

The sod-cutting ceremony started in the grounds of Dundanion Castle, the day's proceedings being enlivened by the band of the 67th Regiment. At 1.30 pm a grand procession led by Lady Deane proceeded to the construction site where, following an incision in the ground, her ladyship dexterously removed the sod with an appropriately-inscribed silver spade. She then placed the first turf in an ornamental wheelbarrow and wheeled it for a short distance, wishing success to the railway to the accompaniment of cheers, gunfire and a spirited rendering of 'God Save the Queen' by the band. Several Directors and the Mayor then emulated Lady Deane's example, after which the official party adjourned to the castle to partake of a sumptious banquet, presided over by Robert O'Callaghan Newenham, deputising for Sir Thomas Deane (1792–1871) the landowner and host who was unavoidably absent.

In all, the sod-cutting ceremony was a great success, and news of the event even reached *The Illustrated London News*, which published a detailed engraving of the assembled dignitaries. Lady Deane and the other ladies were depicted in voluminous crinolines, while many of the gentlemen wore military uniforms. The cream of Cork society were shown in all their early-Victorian finery, though here and there one or two peasant faces could be seen peering incongruously from the background (a reminder to middle class readers that, while Anglo-Irish society could still enjoy such glittering occasions, thousands of ordinary people were starving in southern and western Ireland).

Construction proceeded apace throughout the winter of 1847–48, and by August 1848, fourteen months after the work had started, much of the formation was well advanced. The works included a cutting west of Blackrock station where two accidents occurred, one fatal due to undermined banks having collapsed, while another worker suffered fractured legs when a spoil wagon got out of hand. By the following November, some £16,000 arrears of calls on shareholders were owing, and an Extraordinary Meeting of the Board took place to arrange for the borrowing of £43,000 in order to facilitate the completion of the railway; £15,000 was advanced by the Board of Public Works Commissioners for that purpose.

With a view to the possible doubling of the track at some future date, sufficient land had been acquired for two lines of rails, and as a result of the excessively high prices demanded (to which the Chairman referred pointedly in 1850) the undertaking was destined to cost some £21,000 per mile. However, the company was in a much better position by May 1849, many arrears of calls on shares having been paid; income to 28th April, 1849 totalled £56,181, while expenditure for the same period stood at £46,468.

In order to expedite the completion of the works the CB & PR Directors arranged for the contractor William Dargan (1799–1867) – then engaged on a Great Southern & Western contract between Cork and Mallow – to build the final section of the CB & PR line between Toureen Strand and the Steam Packet quay at Passage.

The employment of William Dargan can be seen, perhaps, as an indication that the Cork Blackrock & Passage promoters were determined to see their scheme brought to a successful conclusion. Although he did little work outside Ireland, Mr Dargan was one of the greatest figures of the Railway Age; an associate of Thomas Telford and Sir John Macneill, this highly-versatile contractor had built railways throughout Ireland ('at this time', declared *The London Journal*, 'Mr Dargan's character was firmly established as a most conscientious and successful contractor', and his name was already 'associated with almost every railway in Ireland').

With the railway at last taking tangible shape in the pleasant County Cork countryside, the CB & P Directors turned their thoughts to operational matters. In order to ascertain the average yearly costs of traffic operation, but particularly to avoid the initial outlay on motive power and rolling stock at a time of monetary stringency, an arrangement was made with John Dawson of the Phibsboro' Coach Works, Dublin, who agreed to provide and operate services on a basis of 100 miles per day at 2 shillings per mile.

Lady Deane, the wife of a prominent CB&PR supporter, cuts the first sod at the ceremony held at Dundanion Castle on 15th June, 1847.

Illustrated London News

The line from Cork to Passage was in a state of near completion by the early months of 1850, and in May the Cork Blackrock & Passage Directors agreed that a trial run could be made with an engine and coaches to test the stability of the new line and works. A special train was therefore run from Passage at approximately 3 o'clock in the afternoon, the western terminus at Cork being reached in 17–18 minutes. It was estimated that the 6¼ mile journey could be performed with ease and safety in about 10–12 minutes, and in fact, at a later period, regular non-stop trains did indeed cover the distance in that time.

The test run was witnessed by large and enthusiastic crowds, and although the CB & PR line was not yet open for public traffic, it appears that the press turned out in force. A detailed report of the new railway appeared in *The Illustrated London News* just a few days later, the text of the report being as follows:

In our Number 269, Vol. 10, for June 1847, we gave a sketch of Lady Deane commencing the Cork Blackrock and Passage Railway by cutting a turf on the grounds of Sir Thomas Deane. We now have much pleasure in returning to the same spot, after an absence of nearly three years, to record the first engine and tender passing over the line.

This event, looked forward to by the citizens for some time past, took place on Tuesday the 14th, and was hailed with delight by the health-seeking as well as recreation-enjoying portion of the community, to whom, as well as the business portion of the citizens, it will be a great boon.

For some time, in the early stages of the works on this line, doubts were entertained as to the chance of its ever being completed; but fortunately, the whole management passed into the hands of a few practical business men, who brought the undertaking to its present state; and that, too, without the aid of loan, or having pressed with severity on the shareholders, and at a considerable amount under the first estimate for the line.

In a few days the passenger traffic will commence, and open, even to the Corkonians, for the first time, glimpses of scenery along the road for which they are little prepared, notwithstanding the many thousand voyages made by steamers up and down the river. After leaving the station at Passage, the line runs close by the side of the public road, and sweeps around Horsehead, showing the beauties of Marino, up to Belveley Bridge, Smith Barry's Bay, the Little Island, and beautifully undulating and planted background of hilly scenery on the right. After rounding Horsehead the line again runs close by the high-road, and shows a broad lake surrounded on all sides by richly planted hills, studded with the mansions of wealthy citizens and country gentlemen; having in the distance Blackrock Castle and the Mathew Testimonial Tower, with a peep at the Glanmire side of the river.

At Stop Island, the rail for the first time crosses the high road and mouth of the Douglas Channel, previous to entering the deep cutting at Blackrock, and shows the Douglas Channel. After passing through the cutting, the line again joins the water, and comes out at Dundanion, as shown in the accompanying sketch, exhibiting at a glance one of the finest views on the river – the busy city, with its tall spires, its smoking chimneys and hundreds of tapering masts, with a broad sheet of water in the forepart of the picture, and the banks of Blackrock, the brickfields, and Glanmire on each side, with the busy splash of the steamer and sluggish move of the deeply-laden emigrant vessel.

From Cork to Passage the line is dead level, and presented no engineering difficulties; save at Blackrock, where a long and deep cutting had to be made so as to reach the mouth of the Douglas Channel, where it again became a labour of filling, and continued on to Horsehead, from which place to the station at Passage a sea wall had to be built, thus to terminate the works for the present.

On Tuesday, the carriages having arrived by the Great Southern & Western Railway, were placed on the rails and sent up and down the line until three o'clock, when a full freight of the Directors and shareholders – as many as could be accommodated on both engine and tender, besides what the carriages could contain – were taken down in 17 minutes and brought back in 10½, performing the run up and down quite to the satisfaction of all, and without the least possible oscillation or disagreeable motion.

Captain Wynne's Inspection

The test run was clearly successful, but before opening the line for public traffic the CB & PR Directors had to obtain government sanction. Acts passed in 1840 and 1842 empowered the Board of Trade to appoint inspecting officers to visit every new line of railway, these gentlemen being recruited from the Royal Engineers. From 1846 until 1851 the inspecting officers reported to a body known as 'The Railway Commissioners' (a sort of Ministry of Transport) but the principle remained the same – that is to say, no new railway could be brought into use until it had been 'passed' by a responsible officer. Thus, on 23rd May, 1850, Captain George Wynne RE arrived in Cork to inspect the works of the Cork Blackrock & Passage Railway.

It is easy to imagine the scene as, accompanied by slightly nervous CB & PR officials, the inspecting officer boarded his special train. Passing slowly along the line, Captain Wynne would have examined every detail with a critical eye – particular attention being paid to underline bridges that might, on a poorly constructed railway, collapse under the weight of a train. Happily, the inspector could find little amiss with the newly-completed line, and after completing his examination of the works he hurriedly wrote out the following report:

23rd May, 1850

Sir,

I have the honour to aquaint you, for the information of the Commissioners, that I have this day inspected 6 miles 23 chains of the Cork Blackrock and Passage Railway between Cork and Passage West.

The formation level and works are constructed for a double line of rails, but at present there is but one line of rails laid down. The principal work on the line is a viaduct 100 yards in length over the Douglas channel. It is constructed on a curve of 60 chains radius and consists of ten openings, ranging from 23 to 28 feet in width, and one opening of 50 ft span. The piers and abutments on piles, and the openings, with the exception of the centre one, are crossed by double baulks . . . the centre opening has wrought iron bottom girders which, with one exception, showed no appreciable deflection.

A great part of the railway is carried on an embankment along the shore and the water of Cork Harbour, and the slopes, which are subject to the action of water, are protected with a sufficient stone pitching.

At this point in his report, Captain Wynne noted that there were several 'deviations in the levels beyond the Parliamentary limits', but he did not consider that these created any problems. He next turned his attention to the condition of the permanent way and other works:

I found the permanent way in good order, the platforms complete, and the signals in course of erection. There are turntables at each end of the line.

I am of the opinion that the line may be opened with safety for the conveyance of passengers, and recommend that the usual certificate be granted.

I am, Sir,
Your servant,
Geo. Wynne, Capt. RE[1]

Captain Wynne would no doubt have informed the Cork Blackrock & Passage officials that the line had successfully passed its inspection, and this good news was passed on to the rank and file CB & PR shareholders at a half-yearly meeting held just one week later. Following this meeting, the Directors and some of the shareholders evidently treated themselves to a run over the new railway in the tender of a borrowed Great Southern & Western engine! It is understood that the engine used on this occasion was GS & WR 2−2−2 No. 2; the engine had probably been hired by William Dargan, and its transference to the physically-isolated Cork Blackrock & Passage line must have been a difficult and lengthy task (the locomotive may have been transported overland from the unfinished Great Southern & Western railhead at Blackpool, though it is perhaps more likely that water transport was used).

Details of the Line

The line from Cork to Passage was officially opened for public traffic on Saturday 8th June, 1850, with the first train leaving Cork at 10 am. Traffic over the newly-opened Cork Blackrock & Passage Railway on its first weekend was colossal, especially on Sunday 9th June, well over 6,000 passengers being carried on that day; one train conveyed no less than 460 persons, while the last service from Passage to Cork at 9.30 pm was packed almost to suffocation! (About a year later, a CB & PR train was said to have carried 800 people.)

The initial train service consisted of 10 trains each way, with fares of 6d. (1st class) and 4d. (second class) for single journeys. At first, no 3rd class accommodation was provided, but it was soon found necessary to add 3rd class facilities – although the company had not originally intended to do so.

At Cork, the CB & PR's City Park terminus was situated at the northern end of Victoria Road, adjoining Albert Quay, and some 12 minutes walk from the city centre at St Patrick's Bridge. A connecting omnibus service was soon introduced – possibly as a result of press correspondence urging that Cork Blackrock & Passage trains should run into the nearby Cork & Bandon Railway terminus. (At that time, however, the latter system had not been completed into Cork.)

Road feeder services were also introduced between Passage and Monkstown, a 'well-appointed' omnibus being provided for first class travellers at a fare of one penny! There were, meanwhile, lingering hopes that the railway might be extended beyond its existing terminus to serve Monkstown directly but although the Cork Blackrock & Passage Directors had obtained an extension of time for completion of the extension, the authorised line between Passage and Monkstown was eventually abandoned.

The new railway was laid with bridge rails weighing 84 lb. per yard; it was single track throughout, and there were no connecting links to other lines. From Cork, the route ran due east across a level tract of land, the first mile being virtually flat. After 1½ miles the single line curved away from the river and passed under two bridges to enter a deep cutting near Dundanion Castle; this excavation had involved the removal of 91,292 cubic yards of rock and earth. Blackrock station was situated towards the southern end of the cutting, and beyond this the route reached its modest summit – which was only 21 ft above the Cork terminus.

From Blackrock, the route continued across the 11-span Douglas viaduct before turning eastwards for the final approach to Passage. Here, the railway ended beside the steamboat pier, run-round and turning facilities being available for locomotives. The pier itself (along with similar structures along the shores of the harbour) was the property of the Cork Harbour Commissioners, although the commissioners had evidently co-operated with the railway company to provide convenient inter-change facilities for the travelling public.

Logically, eastbound workings between Cork and Passage were regarded as down trains while, in the reverse direction, trains from Passage to Cork were up workings. (In this respect the Cork Blackrock & Passage line conformed to the Great Southern & Western system whereby trains to and from Dublin were regarded as up and down workings respectively.)

Broad Gauge Locomotives

The Cork Blackrock & Passage Railway was worked by three small 2–2–2 well tanks, which remained in service for 50 years. Built by Sharp Brothers, they were delivered in 1850, and took the numbers 1, 2 and 3. Nos. 1 and 2 (works Nos. 655 & 656) were ordered on 15th October, 1849, while the third engine was ordered on 14th May, 1850; the three locomotives cost £1,500. Their principal dimensions were as follows:

Cylinders (inside)	12 in. × 18 in.
Driving wheels	5 ft diameter
Leading wheels	3 ft 6 in. diameter
Trailing wheels	3 ft 6 in. diameter
Heating surface	669.1 square feet
Firebox	3 ft long
Well tank	340 gallons

As built, the engines had open footplates, but cabs were eventually fitted. Their livery was light green with yellow and black lining, the domes (with safety valves) being of polished brass, and positioned on the front boiler ring immediately behind the chimneys. They were originally equipped with brakes on the trailing wheels only, but modified brakes were later fitted; No. 2, for example, received clasp brakes on its driving wheels, and all three engines were equipped with vacuum brakes after 1890. No. 2 was subsequently rebuilt as a saddle tank. Further details of the three CB & PR locomotives are supplied by Mr R.N. Clements:

Brakes on hind wheels only when built. Brakes on leading wheels of Nos. 1 and 3 were unusual, also the clasp brakes on driving wheels of engine No. 2. Neither 1 nor 3 had normally-placed handbrakes like No. 2; these were probably originally positioned beside the firebox on the right-hand side, and the projections in front of the cab of No. 3, and side sheet of No. 2's cab were for the wheel. This was not required at the side of No. 3 as the cab is visibly wider than that of No. 2 (it is presumed No. 1 was similar to No. 3 in width). Nor did Nos. 1 and 2 require such fittings in front, as the upper part of the cab is longer than that of No. 3. If this surmise is right it follows that the firebox position was the original one. Actual dates of delivery (presumably dates of leaving maker's works): Nos. 1 and 2 on 1-7-1850, and No. 3 on 16-11-50).

Early Coaching Stock

The Company's small fleet of passenger vehicles eventually comprised three firsts, two seconds, and six thirds, also two composites, and a pair of brake vans; they were either four- or six-wheeled vehicles, and in several instances had the seats arranged around the sides. Unfortunately, their general dimensions are not known, though is of interest to note that according to the company's Chairman Dr Robert Lyons (1826–86) the first of the 3rd class coaches was named 'The Doctor' – presumably as a compliment to him.

The stock was probably built by John Dawson, who had supplied vehicles to other Irish railways, notably the Waterford and Tramore line.

The CB&PR owned two open ballast wagons, but no goods vehicles were provided in the early years. This was, at least in part, because much local goods traffic was carried by steamers on the River Lee, though it is interesting to recall that when a Cork Blackrock & Passage shareholder asked why goods traffic could *not* be developed, he was told that the line was 'too short' to carry goods! There was, on the other hand, a considerable traffic in parcels and other small items that could easily be carried by passenger train, and it seems likely that large quantities of groceries and agricultural produce would have been carried as passengers' luggage on market days.

Mid-Victorian Developments

The Cork Blackrock & Passage Railway operated successfully throughout the summer of 1850. A revised timetable was introduced on 30th September, and this provided eight services each way on weekdays and nine on Sundays; trains from Cork left on the hour while corresponding workings departed from Passage at half-past the hour. Interestingly, the latter were shown as '10½' and '12½' (etc.) trains instead of the more usual '10.30 am' and '12.30 pm' designation.

The weekday trains, and eight of the Sunday workings, had road connections to and from Monkstown, the exceptions being the 11 pm down and the '1½' up workings on Sundays.

On a minor note, it is worth recording that the Cork Blackrock & Passage Directors liked to boast that their railway had been 'the first out of Cork', and in this respect they were entirely correct because the neighbouring Cork & Bandon line was not opened through to its Cork terminus until December 1851. Similarly, the Great Southern & Western Railway originally termin-

CB & PR 5 ft 3 in. gauge 2–2–2 No. 2. This engine was originally a well tank, but it was later rebuilt as a saddle tank as shown here. The curious projection on the cab side sheeting was necessary in order to accommodate the brake wheel, which was too wide for the cab. *Locomotive and General Photographs*

The same locomotive hurries along the line near City Park terminus. The date is probably around 1890–1900. *Locomotive and General Photographs*

ated at Blackpool, on the north side of the city centre – the mile long tunnel to Lower Glanmire Road not being opened until 1855.

By the end of November 1850, the CB&PR had earned a surplus of £1,500, less office ancillary expenses; 79,106 first class, and 119,641 second class passengers had been carried, and 20,000 miles run, the average receipts being £195 per week, though they were expected to fall in winter. Meanwhile, the Directors had decided that the railway could be worked more economically by themselves, and the operating agreement with John Dawson was therefore terminated with effect from 1st June, 1851. From that date, the CB&PR would take over Mr Dawson's engines and rolling stock, payment for this equipment being by instalments; the estimated cost of the engines and other equipment was £9,000.

Details of the new operating arrangements were announced at the halfyearly Cork Blackrock & Passage meeting held in Cork at the end of 1850. This meeting was reported in *The Railway Times* on 7th December, 1850, and part of the Directors' report to the shareholders is quoted below:

> The traffic from the opening of the line on 8th June to the 26th of October last amounted to £3,909, being an average of £195 per week; but as the traffic would fall off during the winter months they did not expect that the receipts would average more than £150 per week, or £7,800 for the whole year.
>
> The Directors are of the opinion that by making proper arrangements and running a greater number of trains than they contracted for to accommodate the public, they would be enabled to develop the resources of the railway and increase the receipts very considerably. They had found it expedient to come to an understanding with Mr Dawson, the contractor for working the traffic, by which on the 1st June next year the company will take the engines, carriages and working stock off his hands and work the line themselves.
>
> The number of passengers conveyed on the railway was 198,747, including 79,106 first class passengers and 119,641 second class passengers. The aggregate number of miles run by the trains was 20,000. The result of working the line for 20 weeks has been to leave a surplus of £1,500, but out of this sum office and other expenses are to be deducted.
>
> The Directors are confident that in their own hands the line will be worked with greater economy than by contract, and by perfecting the communication to Queenstown and other places in connection with the railway the net returns will be such as to give the shareholders a fair and satisfactory dividend on the capital invested.

Sir John Macneill then gave an Engineer's report, in which he stated that the works 'were nearly completed', though more accommodation would soon be needed to cater for 'the Queenstown traffic'. He added that 'the capital account showed that £108,189 had been received and £105,259 expended, leaving a balance of £2,930 in hand'.

In moving the adoption of the report, Dr Lyons explained that the company had been saddled with extra expense as a result of Admiralty requirements at Passage. The average number of passengers carried on the railway had been 10,000 per week, and the trains had run 1,000 miles; the cost of locomotive power and working stock was said to be £100 per week, and this worked out at 'two shillings per mile per train'.

The early 1850s were a time of increased business confidence, and with

CB & PR receipts running at a healthy level, the Directors decided to intro-
duce a steamer service between Passage and Queenstown in connection
with the trains. As the Cork Blackrock & Passage Railway did not possess
powers to operate such services, it was necessary for the Directors and their
friends to form a private company; several of the CB & PR Directors and
shareholders became involved in this novel venture, and William Dargan
subscribed no less than £800 towards the cost of a new vessel.

The Cork Blackrock & Passage Railway's marine subsidiary soon acquired
several small paddle steamers, one of the first being the PS *Queen* (chartered
from the River Steamboat Company). The appearance of these vessels on the
River Lee resulted in fierce opposition from the established shipowners,
who cut their summer fares by 45 per cent, and subsequently the railway
was compelled to reduce its own moderate fares and issue cheap return
tickets.

In November 1850 the Chairman had revealed that the requisite land for
the railway had cost £24,000, further claims for £6,000 being outstanding,
while legal proceedings were pending in respect of the latter. During the
next few years the number of passengers continued to rise; in May 1853 a
further steamer was considered necessary, as a service had been opened to
Ballinacurra near Midleton. It was also intended to seek powers for a railway
between Midleton and Carrigaloe, north of the river, which would be regarded as an extension of the main line; however, nothing further came of
the proposal.

An Exploding Signal

Southern Ireland is not usually regarded as a hotbed of technological
innovation, but Irish railways have, from time to time, initiated developments well *before* their counterparts in England (the Belfast & Northern
Counties Railway, for instance, was a pioneer in the field of motorised road
feeder services). Irish railways have also been used as testbeds for new
equipment, and in this context one might mention a spectacular – if not
overtly dangerous – exploding signal that was installed on the Cork Blackrock & Passage Railway in 1853.

The concept of explosive signalling devices is not as bizarre as it may
appear – after all, detonators are familiar to all railwaymen, while
pyrotechnic signals have long been used at sea. The signal used on the
CB & PR line was, in effect, a combination of these two ideas in that it
attempted to provide both an audible and a clearly visible warning (presumably for use in emergency situations). The experiment was the brainchild of
Captain Norton, a locally-based inventor, and the equipment was described
as follows in *The London Journal* on 24th December, 1853:

> EXPERIMENTAL RAILWAY SIGNALS – At the Cork and Passage (Ireland)
> Railway terminus, a rod of iron was fixed vertically, and on the top of it was tied a
> paper bag containing a pound of blasting powder and sawdust; a slip of slow-
> match was lighted like a cigar with a Vesuvian and quickly drawn up by a cord so
> adjusted as to enter the bag of powder and explode it. The flash from this powder
> would resemble lightening, or the blowing up of an ammunition wagon, so as to be
> seen far and wide.

Captain Norton proposes to have Bengal and other lights attached to the top of the iron rods, which may be instantly raised to their position. The fire of the powder igniting the lights, the flash would attract and fix attention. After this a small paper bag of gunpowder, having a cord passing through it, with the attached slow match ignited, was thrown by the hand upwards into the air. When the bag reached the length of the cord, the lighted match entered and exploded the powder. Captain Norton is preparing a ballista which will throw a bag of powder to a height of fifty feet or more into the air and instantly explode it by the above-mentioned means.

The First CB & PR Steamers

By 1855 the railway's subsidiary steamboat company was operating four paddle steamers. All had been built on the River Thames between 1851 and 1854; the largest vessel was the PS *Victoria*, which was about 134 ft long and had a Gross Registered Tonnage of 111 tons. The PS *Albert* was slightly smaller, with a GRT of 107 tons, while the PS *Queenstown* was around 113 ft long and had a gross tonnage of 81 tons.

The fourth, and smallest steamer was the PS *Fairy*, which was about 95 ft long and had a GRT of just 56 tons. Interestingly, Queen Victoria had sailed from Cove to Cork aboard the 'steam tender *Fairy*' on the occasion of her visit to Ireland in 1849, and it is conceivable that this vessel subsequently passed into CB & PR ownership – although Duckworth & Langmuir[2] suggest that the railway *Fairy* was a slightly later steamer, dating from 1853 (in which case the new vessel must have taken the name of its illustrious predecessor).

A further point which should perhaps be made in connection with the 1849 Royal visit concerns the renaming of Cove which, on 1st August, 1849, had officially been renamed 'Queenstown'. The change of name underlined the growing popularity of this fashionable resort on the north side of Cork Harbour; already an important terminal for the Cork Blackrock & Passage steamers, Queenstown would, in the years to come, emerge as one of the company's most significant cross-river destinations.

The following table provides details of the four paddle vessels operated by the Cork Blackrock & Passage Railway's maritime subsidiary prior to 1881; these steamers were registered in the names of several CB & PR Directors, but they were, for all intents and purposes, 'railway' vessels.

Table 1
VESSELS OPERATED BY CB & PR'S UNOFFICIAL SUBSIDIARY
(PRIOR TO 1881 ACT)

Type	Name	Details
PS	Queenstown	Gross tonnage 81, Length 113 ft beam 15.1 ft depth 6.9 ft, two cylinders. Finally disposed of in 1855.
PS	Victoria	Tonnage 111, two cylinders, 29 in. × 33 in. stroke developing 50 hp. Length 134 ft beam 15.1 ft depth 7.6 ft. Disposed of 1885.
PS	Fairy	Tonnage 56, length 95 ft beam 13 ft depth 7 ft two cylinders.
PS	Albert	Similar to *Victoria*. Tonnage 107, length 133.3 ft beam 15.1 ft depth 7.7 ft. Disposed of in 1882.

Growing Competition

Cut-throat competition between the railway vessels and their rivals resulted in a considerable drop in revenue during the middle 1850s – although the number of passengers had risen by 35,473 in the second half of 1855. This loss of revenue had been caused, in great part, by the need to reduce fares – cheap day returns of 8d. first class and 6d. second class having recently been introduced, together with third class singles to Queenstown at just 2d. At the same time, the railway had itself been allowed to fall into disrepair. The permanent way was said to be in a poor condition, a previous Traffic Superintendent being blamed for this sad state of affairs; his successor had, after carrying out a full track inspection, found it necessary to replace many sleepers and bolts.

At the November 1855 CB & PR half-year meeting the Chairman referred to a possible 'understanding' with the River Steamer Company. It was hoped that an agreement could be made whereby competition might be limited, and in the following year a series of negotiations led to an arrangement between the CB & PR and its opponents. As part of a comprehensive agreement made on 6th May, 1856 an advance of £5,000 (or such proportion as was deemed necessary) was paid to the River Steamer Company by the Cork Blackrock & Passage Railway through its bankers.

There was also provision for certain other payments which possibly related to the activities of the railway steamer undertaking, and these were facilitated by the railway Directors seeking a substantial monetary vote, technically for their services, of which the major part was paid to the River Steamer Company. William Dargan apparently figured in the negotiations and subsequently the railway income increased substantially, although the steamer concern ran competing excursion trips around Cork Harbour on summer weekends.

In 1859, the Cork & Youghal Railway was opened from a city terminus north of the river at Summerhill; this undertaking was to prove a serious competitor of the Passage company because its Board then sought, and obtained, Parliamentary consent for a branch to Queenstown, which opened on 1st March, 1862, under the title 'Cork and Youghal and Queenstown Direct Railway'. As a countermeasure, the Cork Blackrock & Passage Directors arranged for a horse bus to run from the centre of Midleton to Ballincurra, with a ferry connection to Passage. This entailed a long and tedious journey to Cork involving at least two changes, so it is not surprising that the Cork & Youghal Chairman commented 'the people of East Cork and Midleton would sooner travel to the city on a jingle' (a horse-drawn, two-wheeled covered vehicle indigenous to Munster).

Incidentally, at a Board Meeting on 28th November, 1860, it transpired that agreements of October 1856 and October 1860 between the CB & PR and the River Steamer Company had been terminated. It was therefore resolved that at the half-yearly meeting on the morrow, the shareholders would be recommended to vote £400 to the Directors for the purposes of the railway and steamer companies (subject to the latter admitting that the joint agreements were ended) in full settlement of all claims by the steamer company over the period 31st May to 29th November, 1860. This proposal was submitted to the steamer company, without prejudice to the railway company's rights in the event of the proposal being rejected. The terms were, however, fully accepted by the steamer company's proprietors, and co-operation between the CB&PR and the River Steamer Company thereby came to an end.

Competition between the CB&PR and Cork & Youghal Railway soon obliged the Cork Blackrock & Passage Railway to reduce its combined railway-steamer through fares to Queenstown, but within a few years the Cork & Youghal company was in such dire financial straits that the C&YR Directors considered selling or leasing their undertaking to the Great Southern & Western Railway; they even made tentative approaches to the Passage company about a possible merger. At that time the American Civil War was in progress and this caused a CB&PR Director to observe that: 'The situation here is like that in America; the Northerners declared war on the Southerners but, finding that they cannot annihilate us, they will be glad to come to terms'.

Nothing came of the proposed CB&PR/C&YR merger, and in 1866, the Cork & Youghal Railway was purchased by the Great Southern & Western company, which paid £310,000 for the line (considerably less than its original cost). By 1867, the GS&WR had completed a connecting link between its own line at Cork and the Youghal branch, and this enabled trains to run through to the port of Queenstown. The future importance of Queenstown was thereby ensured, and within the next few years, it developed as a major port of call for transatlantic ocean liners.

Reverting briefly to operational matters, three new first class coaches had been added to the Cork Blackrock & Passage Railway's passenger stock in 1861, the original first class vehicles being reduced to 'seconds' while the 'inconvenient old conveyances' that had hitherto been used as seconds became 'thirds'.

The CB&PR line had a good safety record, but on Christmas Day 1863 a mishap occurred to a train 'of immense length carrying 700 passengers' (this figure is much open to doubt) when, due to the load, a coach spring broke and the body settled on top of the wheels. Friction soon caused the woodwork to ignite, which was fortunately observed, and the train stopped; the passengers were duly evacuated, but had to walk the rest of the way to their destinations.

In the previous year, a local newspaper had reported considerable annoyance to passengers when, on reaching Passage station by the 9.45 pm steamer from Glenbrook, they found that the 10 pm train for Cork had departed. When the next train (due to leave at 11 pm) arrived the passengers boarded it, only to be kept waiting for a private party which did not turn up until 11.30, the result being that the train did not reach Cork until 11.50 pm! The journal 'advised' the company's Directors in future to provide a special train for their 'friends' rather than keep 300–400 people waiting for a dozen.

At the May 1865 company meeting, a shareholder referred to the projected construction of new Naval Docks at Haulbowline, and a proposal mentioned some time previously to extend the CB&PR via Monkstown, Ballybrittain, and Ring, to the above place, at a cost of about £60,000. The Chairman confirmed that their line would be suitable for extension, though in order to reach Haulbowline Island an expensive bridge would be needed.

Two years later, in 1867, 450 yards of track near the Cork terminus was renewed at a cost of nearly £500, and other worn and damaged rails were replaced with some of the old metals; many yards of new sidings had also been provided at Cork and Passage stations. (Owing to the work having to be done at night, the cost was much enhanced.) Coaching stock repairs were receiving greater attention in view of the age and wear of the vehicles, but decreased expenditure on engine repairs (two having been re-boilered in 1865) neatly balanced the outlay on the permanent way. Nevertheless there had been other sizeable expenses so no dividend was possible.

In May 1866 the failure of bankers Overend & Gurney resulted in a severe economic crisis which made it increasingly difficult for small railways such as the CB&PR to finance new capital projects. In these circumstances, any plans that may have been tentatively made for an extension beyond the existing terminus at Passage were abandoned.

Despite this setback, the proprietors of the Cork Blackrock & Passage Railway had at least some cause for self-congratulation. They had, for a time at least, come to an agreement with the River Steamer Company, and their modest railway was holding its own in competition with the rival GS&WR branch to Queenstown. All things considered, the Passage line had enjoyed modest success, and its owners could look forward to a prosperous future as Ireland slowly recovered from the traumas of the Famine Years.

The CB&PR Directors – A Further Note

On a footnote, it may be worth adding that, although many of the CB&PR supporters lived in and around Cork, a significant group of shareholders resided in Dublin. This dichotomy was also apparent among the Directors, who lived either in Dublin or Cork. The then Chairman, Robert Hall, and Deputy Chairman, Michael Hayes, came from Cork, but Directors Alexander Findlater, Patrick Jeffers, Nicholas King and John Chinnery Armstrong were Dublin-based. The other Board members – John Sugrue, Charles B. Ware, Timothy Mahony, Edmund Burke, Joseph Carroll and Sir William B. Hackett – lived in the Cork area. These gentlemen remained on the Board for several years, the Directors in 1870 being the same as those in the mid-1860s.

Collectively, the Cork Blackrock & Passage Directors were similar to their counterparts in England in that they were either landowners or wealthy professional men; many of the Board members seem to have had a legal background, though Nicholas King of Dublin was a doctor.

The CB&PR Directors were predominantly Anglicans, and in this respect they were again very similar to their English counterparts (many of whom were members of the Church of England as opposed to non-conformists). In the purely Irish context, the major proprietors of the CB&PR were hardly a representative cross section of local society, although they were probably typical Irish railway proprietors. Indeed, some of the Cork Blackrock & Passage Directors were shareholders in other Irish lines and, as far as the

Dublin-based investors were concerned, the CB & PR would have been merely one of a number of diverse investments; as we shall see, this led to trouble later on, when some of the Dublin men staged a successful boardroom coup.

Notes

1 PRO file MT6 9/101.
2 C.L.D. Duckworth & G.E. Langmuir, *Railway & Other Steamers* (1948),

The 'first locomotive' to pass over the newly-completed CB & PR line at Dundanion in May 1850. The locomotive appears to be a GS & WR 2–2–2. It will be noted that *two* lines are apparently in situ, though one of these may be a temporary contractor's line.   *Illustrated London News*

Chapter Two
Through the Years (1867–1896)

In the early months of 1868 a Parliamentary Bill was lodged by Cork Corporation, the resulting Act (31 & 32 Vic. cap. 33) being known as The Cork Improvement Act. The improvements sanctioned by this Act included the draining of part of Monarea Marshes, together with various other amenities. As far as the Cork Blackrock & Passage Railway was concerned, the proposed changes at Cork involved the removal of a 1½ mile section of the CB&PR line between City Park station and the western end of the Marina, with a diversion along the southern side of a race course giving access to a new terminus in Albert Street.

Proposed Changes at Cork

The Cork Blackrock & Passage Directors were more than happy with the proposed changes at Cork, and speaking at the May 1868 CB&PR meeting the Chairman stated that they favoured the scheme because it would bring the railway terminus nearer to the city centre. Moreover, if the Corporation failed to implement their scheme within two years, or at all, they would be obliged to pay the company £500, while the 50 tons of new rails laid on the old section could be used for renewals elsewhere on the line. In this context the CB&PR company had recently bought £1,437 worth of new rails for cash, in London, comprising the 'plant' of the West Cork Railway Company, at the remarkably low price of £4 18s. 9d. per ton – 'less than any company had ever obtained such rails' – while £503 (£3 2s. 6d. per ton) had been realised on the old metals; in consequence the new rails had cost the CB&PR less than £1,000.[1]

On the subject of rails, it is worth recalling that the Cork Blackrock & Passage line had originally been laid with GS&WR-type bridge rails weighing no less than 84 lb. per yard, but as this original track wore out it was relaid with lighter section 75 lb. per yard Vignoles rails; in November 1867 Mr Barber, the traffic superintendent, had reported that as a result of the heavy traffic carried over the CB&PR the upper surface of the rails had been worn away!

In November 1868 reference was made to the revised departure times of trains from Cork, which now left at the half-hour instead of on the hour; this was expected to please the railway's patrons – especially those travelling to and from Queenstown, where the Great Southern & Western Railway was competing fiercely with CB&PR services. Steamer receipts on the Crosshaven route had risen in the previous year, but the Directors were considering abandoning the service to Ballinacurra.

In the summer of 1869, six sailings daily each way served Crosshaven, the last 'up' steamer leaving at 8.30 pm, while the departure time of the early morning train from Cork had been advanced; moreover, the Aghada route had not been overlooked as regards improved facilities. A large sum had been expended on the PS *Victoria* – new iron stringers having replaced the wooden ones – and she was said to be in better condition than when new.

(Full details of the various steamers are given in *Tables* 1, 2, 3 and 4.) In addition, one of the three CB&PR engines had been 'resuscitated' (i.e. reboilered) at reasonable cost. Expenditure had, by May 1871, been reduced, notwithstanding increased traffic. The permanent way and the Douglas viaduct (which was apparently causing trouble) were still involving much outlay, but expenditure was less than in the corresponding period for 1870.

The trains had run 29,689 miles at 6¾d. per mile (including rolling stock repairs) and well over 139,000 passengers carried, with gross revenue over £4,000; however, it was deemed advisable not to declare a dividend in anticipation of making a substantial disbursement at the autumn meeting following the summer peak traffic – thereby following the custom of recent years. In this context, it should be stressed that the CB&PR line was, by minor railway standards, relatively prosperous; in the second half of 1869, for example, the shareholders had received dividends of 6 shillings per share, this being the equivalent of 3 per cent per annum.

In the event, there was no dividend for the second half of 1871 because of the cost of operating the steamer fleet; the Board was obliged to seek money from the proprietors for maintaining these vessels, and at the same time, it was pointed out that a new coach had recently been charged to the capital account.

Referring to the pending introduction of horse trams in Cork (which, however, had a short life of barely three years) the Chairman opined that this would allow them to do away with the buses, and thus save the company considerable tax (the tramway served the CB&PR, Cork & Bandon, and Great Southern & Western Railway stations, passing through the city centre).

There had, in the interim, been no attempt to start work on the Albert Street deviation, but on 13th May, 1872 an amending Act was obtained, and this permitted a deviation of the route authorised in 1868.[2]

Work on the deviation was in full swing by the summer of 1872, and in this connection the company had issued 2000 preference shares in £20 units. The new line commenced where the line from Blackrock reached the Marina, the precise point being at a metal overbridge later known as the 'Crinoline Bridge' because its spiral stairs were a trap for such garments (this structure existed for 50 years). The route ran south-west past the later Cork Athletic and Show Grounds, then west along the southern side of the racecourse and north-west to Victoria Road, which it crossed (requiring a footbridge); beyond, the line ran parallel to Albert Road and ended at the East side of Albert Street near the Cork & Bandon station. This diversion (1½ miles in length) was single track, and would be laid with completely new rails. The Corporation bore most of the cost of the deviation and new station, which involved great expense as many interests had to be acquired, and claims for disturbance satisfied.

The Corporation had awarded the deviation contract to Mr Joshua Hargreave, and this contractor made good progress with the work. The new terminus at Albert Street was well advanced by November 1872, and with completion scheduled for the early months of 1873, the City Park turntable was moved to the new station – a necessary transfer, but one which caused considerable disruption during the final weeks of operation at the old terminus.

Cork Albert Street was finally opened for public traffic on 6th February, 1873, pilot engines having worked over the track on the previous day to ensure that all was in order. The new station was described as 'a plain serviceable structure, similar in plan to the original one with the usual offices, engine depot and stores, and two spacious roofed platforms'. Designed by Sir John Benson (1812–74) the City Engineer (who had also designed several GS & WR stations and built a number of the riverside piers) it was constructed by Joshua Hargreave under the overall supervision of Peter Roddy, also of the Corporation.

The new terminus was adequate in relation to likely traffic requirements, though it had one regrettable feature in so far as the turntable was located near the station entrance, thereby restricting the circulating area. The opening of the new station was marred, to some extent, by a minor incident that took place in the late afternoon when the engine of the 4.30 pm down train was derailed while being turned, resulting in around 30 minutes delay to the advertised services.

The Later 1870s

By 1875, expenditure on the Douglas viaduct was still necessary annually, but two years later, the Engineer reported that maintenance costs would be halved in the future. A few months previously, the Chairman had reported a new agreement with the steamer company whereby the latter's vessels would cease to call at Passage – thereby giving the 'railway' steamers a free hand on the Queenstown run.

In theory, the railway was supposed to work in connection with the CB & PR steamers, but on one occasion a group of angry travellers complained that a train had started from Passage just as a steamer was arriving, with the result that they had been left waiting on the quay. Concerned at this poor service, the CB & PR Directors decided that, in the event of a claim for compensation, the money would be deducted from the wages of the station master and guard!

In 1877 a new steamer was ordered for £6,500, to replace the PS *Queenstown*, which for some time past had been in poor condition. The Directors resolved to obtain a first-class vessel, and £1,000 towards the cost was sought from the shareholders, the rest of the debt to be paid off by instalments. It was expected that the old steamer would realise around £1,000 on being sold, though in reality this was a wildly optimistic prediction. The new vessel was, like her predecessor, a London-built paddle steamer; named PS *Glenbrook*, she was about 136 ft overall, and had a gross registered tonnage of 96 tons. The *Glenbrook* was said to be the fastest steamer on the river, and also one of the most commodious.

In 1878 normal traffic was reduced owing to trade depression and lack of work at Passage docks. Moreover, it was alleged that the Paris Exhibition had seriously affected excursion traffic, and while this claim may seem doubtful it is clear that large numbers of people who normally stayed by the river or travelled daily 'for the air' had gone to the Continent instead during the summer. In addition, the annual regatta at Glenbrook had not been held, and this had also contributed to a diminuation in levels of first class travel.

The company had appointed a Mr Price – an experienced civil engineer – to examine their line; this had been done to satisfy the Directors and shareholders, and did not imply any want of confidence in the Traffic Superintendent whose technical knowledge encompassed mechanical, rather than civil engineering. In due course, Mr Price made his report, to the effect that everything, and especially the Douglas viaduct, was in good order. Respecting the 'company's' steamers these had paid expenses with a small credit balance over the past two years, but the discarded paddle steamer *Queenstown* had not yet found a purchaser.

The winter of 1878 caused much distress among the workers at Passage Docks, many of whom were laid off. Hitherto these men – many of whom were ship's carpenters – had travelled daily to work by rail, thereby bringing welcome revenue to the CB&PR.

The docks were busy again by May 1880, but it was claimed that fewer men were using the railway to get to work because the Dock Company had recently provided cheap houses for them at Passage. Happily, the following summer produced some fine weather, and as a result of increased leisure travel the Cork Blackrock & Passage Directors were able to report improved financial results at the November half-yearly meeting.

A Further Act of Parliament

As the CB&PR company was pressed for capital a further Parliamentary Bill was deemed necessary in order that a residue of unissued capital could be offered for public subscription. In 1880 the Directors decided to seek new Powers to operate steamers, and the outcome was the Cork Blackrock & Passage Railway Steam Vessels Act of 1881. This new Act enabled the CB&PR to end the arrangements whereby the steamers *Victoria*, *Albert* and *Fairy* were owned by a subsidiary company, and instead the three vessels were taken into direct railway ownership. The 1881 Act also permitted the company to raise an extra £26,000 in shares and £8,600 in loans.

The steamers were an important aspect of Cork Blackrock & Passage operations, because the railway itself was merely a short suburban line with no physical connections to any other system. In these circumstances the steamer routes to Crosshaven, Aghada and elsewhere acted as valuable (albeit expensive) feeders to an otherwise insignificant local railway. It was, on the other hand, possible that the railway could be extended beyond its existing limits to serve Monkstown, Carrigaline or Crosshaven, thereby obviating the need for extensive steamer operations – and allowing the steam vessels to be used on a more flexible (and hopefully more profitable) basis during the summer excursion season. The important service to Aghada and Queenstown would clearly be retained, but any extension of the 6½ mile Cork to Passage railway line was desirable insofar as increased rail facilities would lead to greater residential development, and a corresponding increase in daily commuter traffic.

There were, from time to time, suggestions that the Cork Blackrock & Passage company might finance an extension on its own behalf, but in the

1880s and 1890s government legislation made it possible for cheaply-built tramways or light railways to be built with local authority assistance, and there was in consequence an upsurge in the number of Irish light railway schemes. Two such projects for lightly-constructed tramways were brought before the Cork Grand Jury[3] at this time. Both would have served the Carrigaline district, to the south of the existing CB&PR line, although one of these schemes – which envisaged the construction of a line from Cork via Douglas – was virtually a competing route.

The Cork Blackrock & Passage Directors were reluctant to see the competing line being built, but they showed some interest in the second proposal, which, if successfully completed, would have provided a coastal route commencing at Passage and running via Monkstown, Raffeen and Shanbally. Such a line would have acted as a useful feeder to the CB&PR route, and with this thought in mind the Cork Blackrock & Passage Directors negotiated an agreement with the light railway promoters, under which the sum of £250 was contributed towards the suggested scheme.

Sadly, nothing came of these proposed light railway projects, and the Crosshaven extension – when eventually built – was constructed by the CB&PR company under an Act of Parliament, rather than any of the new (and much cheaper) light railway procedures.

Developments in the 1880s

The Cork Blackrock & Passage line continued to operate much as it had done in the early Victorian period, one innovation being the replacement of the original, mainly-timber Douglas viaduct with a more durable structure. A contract for rebuilding the bridge had been let by the beginning of 1886, and a new first class coach had also been ordered; it was expected that this vehicle would be ready for service by the following summer.

On the administrative side, the 1880s saw various small changes, notably the appointment of J.J. O'Sullivan as General Manager with responsibility for overall traffic development. The line had, for many years, been managed by a Secretary and a locomotive & traffic superintendent, these two officers being responsible for administrative and engineering matters respectively. James Barber had served as CB&PR traffic superintendent for several years, having previously held similar positions on the Londonderry & Enniskillen and other Irish railways; J.J. O'Sullivan, the new General Manager, was formerly the CB&PR accountant. The Engineer, in 1883, was J.W. Dorman – a well known name in Cork Railway circles.

The Passage line was still a relatively prosperous concern, although traffic declined slightly in the 1880s. It was suggested that, if the public could be given greater travel incentives, the level of passenger traffic would increase. Reduced fares were thought to hold the key to improved profitability and accordingly, in October 1885, this expedient was tried, with the result that by December the decline in passengers had been arrested by 5,887 (equal to £128 11s.). The Board was so gratified that it decided to experiment further by abolishing a long-standing grievance – namely the charging of a flat fare irrespective of distance on the steamers, which had penalised pier-to-pier travellers and discouraged short distance travel. Instead of a flat fare, the company built booking offices at each pier and introduced a new, pier-to-pier fare of one penny, with results that surprised the Chairman. Provision was made for a new second class vehicle, the existing one having been declared unfit for further service. The replacement was built by local labour for almost £100 less than an imported coach.

A major row arose at the August half-yearly meeting when John Chinnery Armstrong, a long-serving CB & PR Director who had joined the Board as far back as the 1860s, complained loudly about small dividends and the large payments that were being made in connection with the steamers. He claimed that some Dublin-based stockholders considered that they were getting little or no return on their investments, and after much argument four of the Directors were forced to resign, the vacated positions being filled by four men representing Dublin interests.

Routine repair and maintenance operations continued throughout the 1880s, and in addition to rolling stock replacements and bridge repairs, the company implemented a programme of track renewal. The main line had been completely relaid with steel rails by February 1888, and the sidings were about to be dealt with.

Various improvements had been put into effect at the intermediate station of Blackrock, where the line had been doubled to form a passing loop. The line was now worked on the block and train staff system, and with improved signalling it was possible for two trains to run on the line. For example an 'express' working could follow 15 minutes after a local train, and by connecting with a 'fast' steamer it was possible for through passengers to travel between Cork and the steamer terminal at Crosshaven in just 38 minutes.

Considerable reductions had been made in CB & PR season ticket rates – in some instances by as much as 25 per cent. A shareholder commented on the great increase in passengers (15,000) since 1886, when fares had been higher, while on 15th August, 1888 more passengers were carried than on any previous occasion in the company's history.

It was, around this time, that two important Acts were passed by Parliament. These were the Regulation of Railways Act of 1889, which enforced the use of block working on United Kingdom railways and the fitting of continuous automatic brakes to passenger rolling stock, and the Merchant Shipping (Life Saving Appliances) Act, which imposed stringent regulations compelling shipowners to provide suitable safety equipment. The Regulation of Railways Act was mentioned by the Chairman at a CB & PR half-yearly meeting held on 21st February, 1890; he claimed that the line was 'practically' worked on the block system, but 'supposed' that the company would also have to fit the now-obligatory brake equipment.

Expansion of the Steamer Fleet

The railway's subsidiary steamer fleet had undergone many vicissitudes since the 1850s. As we have seen, the old paddle steamer *Queenstown* had been taken out of service, though the equally-venerable PS *Victoria*, PS *Albert* and PS *Fairy* remained in commission, together with the much newer

PS Albert departs from St Patrick's Quay, around 1900. The masthead pennant proclaims that the vessel is providing an 'excursion' service, while the red ensign flutters proudly at the stern. CB & PR steamers were known locally as the 'Green Boats' because of their livery.

National Library of Ireland

Glenbrook. The *Victoria*, *Albert* and *Fairy* were purchased by the railway company under the terms of the 1881 Act, while the *Glenbrook* – which was delivered in 1881 – apparently passed into direct CB&PR ownership. (Incidentally, the company's vessels were known in Cork as 'The Greenboats' because of their livery.)

Having obtained Parliamentary sanction to operate their own steamer services the Cork Blackrock & Passage Directors were keen to expand their fleet, and in 1882 the 108 ton PS *Monkstown* was delivered. Built by McIlwaine & Lewis of Belfast, the newcomer was about 145 ft long and was powered by a 50 horse power simple expansion engine. The original *Albert* was withdrawn in 1882, a replacement vessel having been built by McIlwaine & Lewis; a 140 ft paddler, the new steamer utilised the *Albert's* engines, and was also named *Albert*.

In retrospect, the year 1890 was a milestone in the company's history. On 31st January an extraordinary meeting of the Citizen River Steamer Company was held on their vessel the PS *Erin*, and at that meeting the proprietors learned that, due to an inability to meet liabilities, the company was being voluntarily wound up. In this way, the CB&PR's principal shipping rivals quietly passed out of existence. The railway company then bought up the defunct concern's assets, paying £1,405 2s. 3d. for a four-vessel fleet consisting of the paddle steamers *Erin*, *Citizen*, *Lee* and *City of Cork* – all built in the 1860s. Of these, Fayle stated that the last-mentioned was 'a splendid old paddle steamer, but far too expensive to run for any length of time with economy'.[4]

At the half-yearly CB&PR meeting held on 22nd August, 1890, in reference to the above deal, it was claimed (obscurely) that it was a matter for 'gratification', not only to the travelling public, but also to the shareholders, that they were thus relieved of one source of river opposition. Moreover, what might not be appreciated was that the public should be *indebted* to the company for their action because the former operators did not provide the same facilities as the railway company; for example, Aghada had been almost deserted for several years past, yet this year had had many summer residents. Credit was also due to the company for not increasing steamer fares following the acquisition, which some people had said might take place.

A new goods vessel – the *Rostellan* – was on order from Messrs McIlwaine & McColl. She would be moderate in cost, capable of high speed, yet would burn only half the amount of fuel used by the present vessel; in addition, her certificate would include the carriage of passengers, if necessary.

Although primarily a goods vessel, the *Rostellan* broke new ground in so far as she was a screw-propelled steamer as opposed to a paddle steamer. The new steamer was a little over 94 ft long, and had a gross registered tonnage of 82 tons. Built of steel, she had 60 horse power engines.

A further steamer, the 85 ton paddle steamer *Queenstown* (II) joined the CB&PR fleet in 1892. Like the *Rostellan*, she was a steel screw steamer from McIlwaine & McColl of Belfast; her 4-cylinder engines developed about 60 horse power, and her length was around 92 ft.

There were, by the early 1890s, no less than five CB&PR steamships in service, the composition of the fleet around 1892 being as shown in *Table 2* (below).

Table 2
CORK BLACKROCK & PASSAGE STEAMERS c.1892

Vessels purchased after 1881 Act, following the conferring of statutory powers on the railway company to own and operate steamers.

Type	Name	Notes
PS	*Glenbrook*	98 tons, built at Poplar, London 1877. Length 136 ft, beam 15 ft, depth 7 ft. Cargo vessel. Disposed of in 1903.
PS	*Monkstown*	Built by McIlwaine and Lewis, Belfast. Similar to *Albert* (II) but having single expansion engines. Length 145 ft, beam 16 ft, depth (moulded) 7.9 ft. Two engines, direct oscillating cylinders, 30 in. × 33 in. stroke. Combined HP 50. Gross registered tons, 108. Sold April 1910.
SS	*Rostellan*	Built by McIlwaine and McColl (1891). Two sets of compound engines, cylinders, 4 ft 7½ in. and 14 in. diameter × 9 in. stroke. HP 17 nominal, 60 indicated. Length 94.5 ft, beam 15.5 ft, depth 6 ft 4 in. Gross tons, 82. Used for freight and passenger work. Sold 1926.
PS	*Albert* (II)	Builders McIlwaine & McColl. Length 140.5 ft, beam 15.5 ft, depth 7.8 ft, cylinders 16 in. × 32 in. diameter × 30 in. stroke. HP 42 nominal (220 indicated).
SS	*Queenstown* (II)	Built by McIlwaine and McColl, Belfast. Twin screw, four engines, inverted cylinders compound. Cyls: 2 7 in. and 14 in. bore × 9 in. stroke. HP 17 nominal, 60 indicated. Length 92 ft, beam 16 ft 6 in., depth 6.5 ft. Net Registered tons 42.56. Gross Registered tons 85. Disposed of in 1925.

The CB&PR paddle vessel *Glenbrook* alongside City Park station. The large sign affixed to the side of the station proclaims that the premises were 'To Be Let or Sold', and the date is therefore after the closure of the terminus in 1878. The new CB&PR terminus at neighbouring Albert Street was very similar to the old one, both stations being Italianate-style structures with adjoining train sheds.

Cork Milling Co., by permission of W. McGrath

In addition, the company owned the former Citizen River Steamer Company vessels *Citizen*, *Lee*, *Erin* and *City of Cork*, but these veteran steamers were soon disposed of, the first three being scrapped between 1890 and 1893, while the City of Cork had been sold in 1890. The four ex-Citizen River Co. vessels purchased by the CB & PR are shown in *Table 3*:

Table 3
CITIZEN RIVER COMPANY VESSELS

(Bought in 1890; all paddle vessels.)

Type	Name	Notes
PS	City of Cork (II)	Gross tons 94. HP 75. Length 150.9 ft, beam 17 ft, depth 6.9 ft. Built by G. Robinson and Co. Cork, 1866. Disposed of 1890.
PS	Citizen	Gross tons 74. HP 80. Length 160 ft, beam 17.7 ft, depth 7.1 ft. Built by Blackwood and Gordon Port Glasgow, 1861. Scrapped 1891.
PS	Lee (II)	Particulars same as Citizen. Disposed of by 1893.
PS	Erin (II)	Gross tonnage 89 (formerly *Rosneath* ex-*Rosalie*). Disposed of 1890.

A point which might be made in relation to the above-mentioned steamers concerns their dimensions. The length of a ship can be measured between perpendiculars or 'overall', but secondary sources do not always indicate which form of measurement is being quoted, and to prevent confusion it should be stressed that the figures given here are approximate. An even greater problem emerges with respect to gross registered tonnage – which is a measure, not of weight but of the capacity of certain enclosed parts of a merchant ship – modifications made during the life of a particular vessel could alter her GRT and confuse subsequent historians! The figures given are therefore open to several interpretations, though it is hoped that the data quoted will at least give readers an idea of the comparative size of each vessel.

Late Victorian Changes

In the early 1890s the CB & PR Directors announced that the erection of a new goods store at 'a convenient point' (which turned out to be Aghada) was envisaged, and a new 'station' (i.e. steamer calling place) was to be built at East Ferry, where the residents proposed instituting a daily road service to and from Ballincurra in connection with the morning steamer.

The Cork Blackrock & Passage Railway may have been an important local steamer operator, but it was also a railway company, and although much time and energy was sometimes devoted to marine business, the railway was certainly not neglected. By 1892, for example, the trains had been fitted with continuous automatic brakes at a cost of £1,500. The goods store and waiting room at Aghada was completed by August, also a tramway to bring goods along the pier, and it transpired subsequently that a sizeable amount of traffic was obtained from local people.

August 1892 saw the announcement of the opening of a central office and store at St Patrick's Bridge for the reception of goods as from 30th September. Additionally, the company, in a desire to encourage tourists from England, had distributed a pictorial poster in London and other large towns advertising Trabolgan Bay, on the east side of Cork Harbour. In association with the estate owners they had opened up this area – a region hitherto unexplored by Cork people – and a coach service was being introduced between Aghada and Trabolgan, while the existing service to Cloyne and Ballycotton was being improved.

The railway system in and around Cork had developed in a somewhat piecemeal fashion, with the Great Southern & Western Railway on the north side of the River Lee and a collection of much smaller railways to the south and west. The most ambitious of these minor lines was the Cork & Bandon[5] which, in 1888, had adopted a more expansive title – 'The Cork Bandon & South Coast Railway'. There had been proposals for a merger of the Cork & Macroom Direct line and the Cork Blackrock & Passage Railway with the Cork & Bandon system, but the latter would not reciprocate, particularly in the case of the CB&PR, on the grounds that no physical connection existed between the two systems. This was, however, a very poor excuse because, although the termini faced in differing directions, it would have been a relatively simple task to lay a connecting spur for through working via the Cork & Bandon goods yard and thence across Albert Street to the Cork Blackrock & Passage station.

By the summer of 1895, the steamer *Glenbrook* had been hired out for trading on the Blackwater River, subject to a season's approval. For some time, the CB&PR Directors had held the opinion that, if fewer steamers were in operation, there would be better prospects of paying an increased ordinary dividend. Indeed, earlier in the year, the Directors had given very serious and lengthy consideration to the heavy expense of maintaining the steamers, which were regarded as a weak point in CB&PR operations. Had it been possible to extend their use over the whole year they would have proved less of an incubus, yet drastic reduction of the fleet would result in the company being unable to meet the heavy summer demand.

The question of an alternative to the steamers inevitably arose; the railway by itself was remunerative, and its extention to Crosshaven was looked upon as a feasible solution which would lead to development of the area for residential traffic. The company's Engineer was therefore instructed to survey a possible route and, following careful analysis of the survey, the General Manager was asked to report on the traffic likely to accrue from such an extension. His findings were then submitted to the General Manager of a Northern Ireland railway which had some features in common with the Cork Blackrock & Passage line. Following a thorough inspection of the site and an investigation into the working of the company, this gentleman reported that in view of the heavy capital and working costs of the steamers, as against the remunerativeness of the railway section, the proposed extension would appear to offer every hope of success. While it would be unwise to abandon the steamer services in their entirety, the extension would enable them to be reduced to a minimum commensurate with efficient operation.

The gauge of the proposed Crosshaven extension was then considered, and finding that if it was laid to the narrow gauge of 3 ft, over £30,000 would be saved, the CB & PR Directors decided that the new line would be a narrow gauge route; as the Cork Blackrock & Passage line was an isolated system with no physical connection to other Cork lines, it was agreed that the existing section between Cork and Passage would also be narrowed.

Thus, in the mid-1890s, a momentous decision was taken – a decision which, when implemented, would alter the CB & PR out of all recognition; after 50 years of successful operation on the 5 ft 3 in. gauge, the Cork Blackrock & Passage Railway was about to become a narrow gauge line! As a corollary of this decision it was hoped that a re-gauged Cork Blackrock & Passage line might, one day, be linked to the Cork & Muskerry Railway[6] thereby enabling CB & PR trains to run through to Blarney and other places served by the Cork & Muskerry system. As we shall see, this interesting project was to get no further than the planning stage, but it is possible that the idea of such a link-up may have been implicit in the Cork Blackrock & Passage narrowing scheme.

A Suggested Tramway Connection

While on the subject of the proposed Cork & Muskerry connecting line it is interesting to recall that, some 20 years earlier, the opening of the Cork Tramways system had prompted suggestions that this horse-worked 5 ft 3 in. gauge line would be pressed into service as a link between the Great Southern & Western, Cork Blackrock & Passage and Cork & Bandon systems. Built by English interests under an Order in Council made in October 1871, the tramway was opened on 12th September, 1872; it ran from the GS & WR terminus on the north side of the River Lee to Victoria Quay on the south side, passing near the terminii of both the Bandon and Passage Companies.

The Cork & Bandon Directors were acutely conscious of their isolation from the rest of the Irish system, and, eager to grasp the opportunities offered by the new tramway they arranged for a siding to be laid into the C & BR goods yard. This facility was used – albeit for a short time – to expedite the movement of fish traffic between west Cork and Dublin. Some parcels or 'smalls' traffic from the CB & PR may also have been trans-shipped onto the tram line, but sadly, the tramway had a very short life, and it was never fully developed as a cross-river link to the GS & WR main line.

Notes

1 Opened from Bandon to Dunmanway on 12th June, 1866, the English-owned West Cork line eked out an impecunious existence as a subsidiary of the Cork & Bandon Railway.

2 In October 1867 the government sent up a special commission to investigate the condition of the Irish railway system with a view to possible nationalisation. This contributed to a period of uncertainty in which many railway projects were suspended until the government's intentions were made clear – which may, at least in part, explain the lack of progress vis-à-vis the Albert Street deviation.

3 Irish 'Grand Juries' were local authorities analogous to the later county councils.

4 H. Fayle, The Cork Blackrock & Passage Railway, *Railway Magazine*, December 1909.

5 Incorporated in 1845, the Cork & Bandon Railway was completed throughout to Bandon in 1851. It worked a number of smaller lines, including the West Cork Railway and the Ilen Valley line.

6 Opened from Cork to Blarney in August 1887, the 3 ft gauge Cork & Muskerry system eventually developed into a relatively complex system, with branches to Coachford and Donoughmore (the latter being owned by a subsidiary company). The story of this obscure line is told in *The Cork & Muskerry Railway* by A.T. Newham (Oakwood Press), republished as a new enlarged edition in 1992.

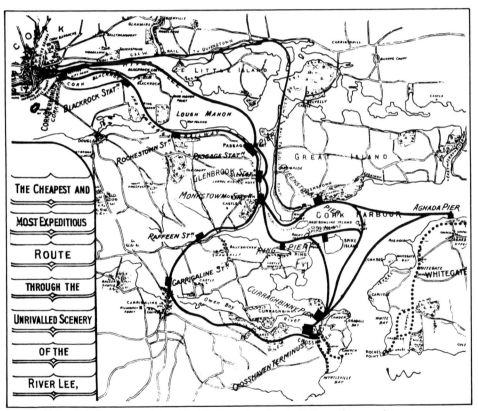

A contemporary map of the CB&PR line, showing both the railway and its steamer 'feeder' routes to Aghada, Queenstown and elsewhere.

Monkstown steamer pier photographed from the adjacent station footbridge; Great Island can be seen in the distance.

National Library of Ireland

Chapter Three
Conversion to 3 ft Gauge (1896–1912)

Before starting work on the proposed Crosshaven extension the Cork Blackrock & Passage Directors had to obtain Parliamentary consent, and in due course steps were taken to lodge the necessary Bill. Among the Powers sought were (a) authorisation to extend the existing railway; (b) permission to extend the area in which the CB & PR company could operate its steamers; and (c) Powers to raise the capital needed to build the extension by means of mortgages and further share issues. It was, at the same time, suggested that the company's name should be officially changed, but in the event this alteration was not implemented.

The Act of 1896

The Bill passed through Parliament in 1896, and on 7th August the Act 'to authorise the Cork Blackrock and Passage Railway Company to extend their Railway to Crosshaven' received the Royal Assent. The new Act allowed the company to raise further capital of £110,000 in shares and £35,000 by loan (though only £80,000 in shares and £26,000 by loan was actually raised).

For convenience, the route of the proposed Crosshaven extension was treated as three railways, the various sections being carefully defined as follows:

> A railway (hereinafter called Railway No. 1), two miles and 6.37 chains in length, commencing in the Townland of Pembroke, in the Parish of Marmullane, in the County of Cork, at a point on the Company's railway at Passage, and terminating in the Townland of Monkstown (Castle Farm), in the Parish of Monkstown, in the said County of Cork.
>
> A railway (hereinafter called Railway No. 2), three miles, three furlongs and 6.63 chains in length, commencing by a junction with Railway No. 1 at the point of termination thereof, and terminating at Carrigaline, in the Townland of Carrigaline (Middle), in the Parish of Carrigaline, in the said County of Cork.
>
> A railway (hereinafter called Railway No. 3), four miles, two furlongs and 0.60 chains in length, commencing by a junction with Railway No. 2, at the point of termination thereof, and terminating at Crosshaven, in the Townland of Knocknagore, in the Parish of Templebreedy, in the said County of Cork.

The CB & PR company was empowered to 'make and maintain' the authorised railway, together with 'all proper stations, sidings, approaches, works and conveniences connected therewith'; the new line would, moreover, 'be constructed and maintained . . . for the conveyance of passengers, as well as goods and animals on a gauge of three feet'.

Further clauses dealt with the complex relationship between the railway company and local landowners, and in this context several extra responsibilities were laid upon the CB & PR. At Carrigaline, for example, the company would have to 'provide and thereafter maintain for the free use of the public' a means of access between 'the public road at Carrigaline and the land lying between Railway No. 3 and the River Owenaboy . . . by means of an accommodation bridge under the railway'. Similarly, the railway company would have to make sufficient provision for the flow of water in all waterways,

A C T

To authorise the Cork, Blackrock and Passage Railway Company to extend their Railway to Crosshaven ; and to confer further powers on the Company in relation to their Undertaking ; and for other purposes.

[ROYAL ASSENT, 7TH AUGUST, 1896.]

WHEREAS by the Cork, Blackrock and Passage Railway Act, 1846 (in this Act called "the Act of 1846"), the Cork, Blackrock and Passage Railway Company (in this Act called "the "Company") were incorporated and authorised to make a railway 5 from the Borough of Cork to Passage West, in the County of Cork: *Preamble.*

9 & 10 Vict., cap. cxlviii.

And whereas by the Cork, Blackrock and Passage Railway Extension to Monkstown and Amendment Act, 1847, the Company were authorised to extend their railway to Monkstown, in the said County of Cork, and to abandon the construction of a certain portion of their 10 authorised railway, and other provisions were made in relation to the Company's undertaking, but such extension to Monkstown was never constructed: *10 & 11 Vict., cap. lix.*

And whereas by the Cork Improvement Act, 1868 (in this Act called "the Act of 1868."), certain alterations of the railways of the 15 Company were authorised, which have since been made: *31 & 32 Vict., cap. xxxiii.*

The title page of the Cork Blackrock & Passage Railway Act of 7th August, 1896, by means of which the CB&PR Company obtained Parliamentary consent for its extension from Passage to Crosshaven.

channels and culverts where they were crossed or affected by the new line, and furthermore, any such waterways or culverts built by the CB&PR should be constructed and finished 'to the satisfaction of the Harbour Commissioners'.

If, for any reason, the railway company failed to fulfil its obligations in respect of access to the river or other matters relating to Cork Harbour, the Harbour Commissioners were empowered to refer any dispute to the Board of Trade, who would appoint an engineer to arbitrate between the two parties. Conversely, the Cork Blackrock & Passage Railway might itself call upon the BoT to settle future disputes, but in general the cost of all works required by the Harbour Commissioners would fall upon the railway company, and the Act clearly stated that the cost of 'all works . . . required to be executed by the Company shall be carried out at their own expense'.

The Work Begins

In engineering terms the Passage to Crosshaven line presented several problems. The authorised route commenced at Passage and ran southwards to Monkstown before turning south-west towards Carrigaline, from where the line ran more or less due east to its destination; the total distance, from Passage to Crosshaven, was 9 miles 64 chains.

Large viaducts would be necessary at Crosshaven and across the Owenboy (or Owenaboy) river near Carrigaline, while at other places the proposed line ran in close proximity to Cork Harbour or the Owenboy estuary. As we have seen, the 1896 Act contained strict provisions in relation to the waterside sections of the proposed extension, but there would, in addition, be minor problems in terms of flood protection – and for this reason much of the extension line would have to be carried on low embankments. Otherwise, the most significant engineering feature would be a tunnel at the northern end of the route near Passage station.

The capital needed for the Crosshaven extension had been partially subscribed by the end of August 1897, and it was reported that every step was being taken to ensure an early start on the new line. Several of the landowners en route to Crosshaven had agreed to the CB&PR company taking possession of the requisite land at an early stage, and this was expected to expedite the work of construction.

Twelve months later, in August 1898, work on the Crosshaven extension was said to be making good progress, the contractor being John Best of Leith. Interestingly, the Cork Blackrock & Passage Directors had considered the possibility of working their new line as an electric tramway, and an electrical engineering firm had investigated this matter very thoroughly. They had even submitted a tender but, after much deliberation, the CB&PR Directors decided not to proceed with the electric traction scheme; instead, they agreed that the Cork Blackrock & Passage line would be completed as a conventional, steam-worked narrow gauge route.

Having rejected the idea of electric traction the company placed orders with Messrs Neilson Reid & Co. of Glasgow for four 2–4–2 tank locomotives, to be built to the maker's own design. Further contracts were placed

Carrigaline viaduct had two main girder spans, each of about 70 ft. There was also a small subsidiary span of around 12 ft (*extreme right*). *Walter McGrath*

The 4-span girder viaduct at Crosshaven was the largest bridge on the line; each span was a little over 75 ft in length. *Irish Railway Record Society*

with Brown Marshall & Co. of Birmingham for the supply of new 3 ft gauge rolling stock.

In the meantime, work on the extension had run into a series of problems, some of them minor, but others of a more serious nature. The CB & PR Board and company officials, together with Mr James the contractor's Engineer, had inspected the works but they were dissatisfied with the rate of progress, and could only hope that the scheduled date for completion (3rd March, 1900) would be adhered to. Certain matters in dispute between the contractor and the railway company's Engineer had been submitted to arbitration. Tenders were being sought for re-gauging the existing Cork–Passage line, and if these were not satisfactory the company would undertake the work with its own staff. It was believed that when this had been completed and the stations re-arranged, a very large traffic could be easily handled without discomfort to passengers.

February, 1900 saw the Crosshaven line very far indeed from completion. The main cause of delay was the boring of the 1,500 foot tunnel between Passage and Glenbrook during which a spring had been encountered midway, much time and expense being involved before this problem was mastered. On the other hand, it was reported that the track between Glenbrook and Monkstown was almost ready, and Carrigaline station was finished, with the usual offices and equipment, together with a passenger subway. Most of the bridges had been erected, and the piers of Crosshaven viaduct were already in place. Meanwhile, revenue was much reduced in relation to the same period in 1899 – principally in consequence of an extension of the Cork Electric Tramways; this concern opened late in the 1890s to Ballintemple, the eastern end running parallel to the railway – and thus depriving it of a good deal of commuter traffic to and from Blackrock.

To aggravate the situation still further the tramway company was promoting a Bill in Parliament for a continuation of their own line as far as Blackrock. Alarmed at this renewed attack on its monopoly, the Cork Blackrock & Passage company strongly opposed the tramway extension scheme, but without success; the tramway Act was passed and the rival line was soon under construction.

While work continued on the Crosshaven extension, the CB & PR was conscious of the need to improve traffic receipts on its existing line, and to encourage people to use the railway, reduced fare weekly tickets for workmen were introduced between Cork and Passage. It was hoped that these tickets would foster trade at the Docks, and also at Haulbowline, while encouraging speculative builders to provide new housing developments alongside the river and harbour.

Financial Problems

Conversion of the existing railway to narrow gauge was being carried out by the company's own staff without altogether disrupting traffic (actually a third rail was laid initially, followed by the piecemeal replacement of one side of the running track); in addition, the Cork–Blackrock section was doubled, the only instance of this on an Irish narrow gauge system. Consideration had been given to doubling the remainder, but this was precluded by financial conditions, the new rails between Blackrock and Passage being laid, for the most part, on the old broad gauge sleepers.

It was, by this time, clear to all concerned that the Crosshaven extension would involve far greater expenditure than had been anticipated. The physical difficulties encountered during the construction of Passage tunnel were bad enough, but on top of these engineering problems there were serious financial troubles – the CB & PR company having been unable to place the remaining £38,600 in shares authorised by the 1896 Act. In these melancholy circumstances the relationship between John Best and the company began to deteriorate, and on 28th July, 1900 the contractor ceased work on the new line to Crosshaven. Litigation followed, and as a result an arbitrator was called in to settle the conflicting claims.

With the works languishing unfinished, special CB & PR shareholders' meetings were held in Dublin and Cork on 2nd August and 17th August respectively, to see how further capital could be raised; it was stressed that unless extra money could be provided, there was grave danger of the outlay to date (£21,000) being lost and the extension becoming derelict. The situation was regarded as essentially one for assistance by the Public Works Commissioners by way of a loan; interviews had already taken place, with a favourable reception, but the terms laid down were onerous and could not be modified without Treasury consent – which would be difficult to obtain. Eventually £65,000 was advanced at 4 per cent interest, as a first charge on the undertaking.

Meanwhile the four narrow gauge engines had arrived and been paid for, but the builders (Brown Marshalls) of the 12 bogie coaches, now completed, would not deliver them until payment was forthcoming. Fortunately, by November 1900, agreement had been reached whereby the railway company would pay £1,154 annually, in quarterly instalments over seven years, the vehicles remaining the property of the builders until fully paid for.

Sunday 29th October, 1900 saw completion of the gauge conversion between Passage and Cork; the line was closed all day, and passengers were carried by steamers. Several trial runs were made that afternoon, on one of which, at 3 pm, the Chairman and Directors participated. The turntable beside the concourse at Albert Street was removed, thereby permitting an enlargement of the circulating area, and a new island platform (in addition to those already existing) was installed, thus providing three terminal tracks with a fourth to be used for carriage storage. In addition, an outlet was opened on to Albert Quay. The rolling stock repair shops were transferred to Passage, and a large goods store was to replace them. The last broad gauge train had left Passage for Cork at 9.30 pm on the Saturday night. The final tally of broad gauge stock was 13 coaches and four wagons. (Some of the redundant 5 ft 3 in. gauge coaches found a new lease of life as platelayers' huts and PW stores).

By 1901, the tramway extension to Ballintemple was proving a very serious competitor to the railway while the engineer Francis Fox, MICE (who had arbitrated in the matter of the award to Best) recommended that the contractor should receive £31,554 in cash, plus 4 per cent interest from

28th July to 31st December, 1900. The award also included materials, costs and other items that had not yet been assessed but were expected to amount to £2,500. Lengthy negotiations ensued in Edinburgh (where Mr Best resided) and in London, and as a result the company offered to increase the payment to £33,364, mainly in 4 per cent debentures, which were to be raised under a new Bill then before Parliament, provided the contractor undertook to complete the railway to the company's satisfaction and ensured its being passed by the Board of Trade.

The Bill previously mentioned was to facilitate the raising of further capital totalling £125,000 (including the hoped-for £65,000 Loan from the Board of Works Commissioners) and to extend the time allowed for completing the Crosshaven extension. The Bill was duly passed, and it received the Royal Assent on 9th August, 1901; subsequent negotiations with Mr Best having been successful, he resumed work on the line in October. Previously, the three old engines and three wagons had been sold, but unfortunately there was only a small balance to hand from the half-year's working at the end of June and this, with an earlier balance, was utilised to pay interest on the 4 per cent first debenture stock, shareholders in other categories receiving nothing.

On 24th January, 1902, Passage tunnel was finally pierced with an 8 foot heading, excavation from the Glenbrook end having commenced in 1900. The firm of Sir Douglas Fox and Partners were consulting engineers to the company, and they were pressing the contractor to expedite the work so that the 2 mile 6 chain Passage–Monkstown section could be opened early in the summer. A year previously, the railway company had been in serious difficulties; the Parliamentary Bill was threatened, legal actions were pending, and several creditors were pressing claims; moreover a large amount of money was owing to the Bank. Happily, the bank overdraft was subsequently paid off, and when Mr Best agreed to accept debenture stock in payment of his award, the company's position improved immeasurably.

Much of the Glenbrook to Carrigaline section had been completed by 1902, and contractor's engines and wagons were able to work over the major portion of the line. In this context it is interesting to record that although the engines ordered from Neilsons did not arrive in Cork until 1900, John Best had used his own locomotives and rolling stock on the unfinished line. At least two engines were used on the Crosshaven extension contract, both of these being 0–4–0 saddle tanks. One of the 0–4–0STs was named *Crosshaven*, but the other was apparently un-named; *Crosshaven* was a Hudswell Clarke product (Works No. 1480) dating from 1897, while its companion was an Andrew Barclay engine (Works No. 297) built in 1887.

Completion of the Works

The section of line from Passage to Monkstown was inspected by Colonel von Donop of the Board of Trade on July 1902, and his report[1] contains many useful details. The deepest cutting on the new section was 23 ft and the highest embankment stood 12½ ft above local ground level; Passage Tunnel was 535 yds long and the 'only real gradient' was 1 in 76.

The BoT Inspector examined the stations in some detail, and some of this information may be worth quoting. The new station at Passage for example, was described as follows:

> At this point an entirely new station has been constructed on a site close to the previously existing one. It is provided with a single platform 405 ft long, 3 ft high and of sufficient width; it has a booking office, waiting room and all suitable accommodation. There is a loop just outside the station but it is not provided with platforms and should not be used for passing passenger trains. A new signal cabin has been constructed, containing 15 levers, of which 2 are spare.

Glenbrook, the next station along the line from Passage, was a much smaller affair, but like all Cork Blackrock & Passage stations it was equipped with a raised platform and a small building:

> The station at this point, which is only half a mile from Passage, consists of a single platform 420 ft long, 3 ft high and 8 ft maximum width. It is provided with a booking office and waiting shed, but with no other accommodation; the company represents that very little traffic is expected at this station, and they agree to provide, at a later date, additional accommodation if it is considered necessary by the Board of Trade. On this condition the existing arrangements may, I think, be accepted for the present.

Colonel von Donop recommended several small improvements on the new line, including 'lamps with names' at all stations and additional ballast in certain places. Otherwise, he was more than satisfied with the completed works, and the new line was 'passed' for opening. The Passage to Monkstown section was accordingly opened for public traffic on 1st August, 1902, and a further portion of the new line was brought into use on 15th June, 1903 when trains began running to and from Carrigaline over an additional 3 miles 36 chains of completed line.

These piecemeal openings took place much later than scheduled, but the company's financial position had decidedly improved. Revenue over the recent half-year had risen by £253, and working expenses were £811 down. Further encouragement came from the Board of Works which had granted £13,568 of the £65,000 loan while, after so many delays, good progress was being made on the final 4 miles 20 chains of line between Carrigaline and Crosshaven.

Opening to Crosshaven

Early in 1904 the company, in anticipation of the imminent opening to Crosshaven, was planning its future train service – and it was claimed that this would be both frequent and regular. Steamer services, which now operated from Monkstown instead of Passage, would continue serving Ringaskiddy, Haulbowline, Queenstown, Aghada and Crosshaven, while in summer an excursion vessel would sail to and from St Patrick's Bridge.

The Carrigaline to Crosshaven section was substantially complete by the spring of 1904. On 17th May Colonel von Donop returned to County Cork to inspect this final part of the extension route, and his report[2] is another mine of information. The largest works included the viaduct at Crosshaven with

The first train through to Crosshaven on 1st June, 1904. The six-coach formation includes four ordinary thirds and two first class observation brakes (distinguishable by their plate glass windows).   *Locomotive and General Photographs*

Crosshaven station, looking towards the buffers; the small waiting shelter visible behind the signal box is not shown on any of the later photographs.   *A.T. Newham*

RAILWAY STATION. CROSSHAVEN. 8853. W.L.

A panoramic view of Crosshaven station during the Edwardian period. The standard CB&PR corrugated iron station building is clearly visible to the right. A variety of equipment can be discerned, including two 'what-the-butler-saw' machines (below the canopy) and a chocolate-vending machine.

National Library of Ireland

four 75½ ft spans; this impressive structure consisted of lattice girders on brick abutments.

At Crosshaven the line ended beside a 200 yds long platform with 'a line on either side for both arrival and departures'; the platform was 25 ft wide and 3 ft high. Crosshaven signal cabin had 24 levers including 5 spares.

In general, Colonel von Donop was pleased with the strength and stability of the new works, and having passed its BoT inspection the Crosshaven extension line was ceremonially opened on 1st June, 1904.

After so many vicissitudes, the Cork Blackrock & Passage Directors were understandably keen to celebrate the completion of their extended line, and 1st June, 1904 was, in truth, a 'red letter day' in the history of the railway. Although the CB & PR was, even in its lengthened form, no more than a local branch line, the railway's supporters arranged a lavish opening ceremony – the guest of honour being no less a personage than the Lord Lieutenant of Ireland, William Ward, the second Earl Dudley (1867–1932); young, handsome, and an extremely popular figure, Lord Dudley was the King's own representative in Ireland,[3] and his presence added an element of grandeur to the Opening Day festivities.

The Royal Navy, too, was called upon to play its part on the Great Day, and through the courtesy of Rear-Admiral McLeod, of Haulbowline Naval dockyard, a supply of flags and bunting was provided to decorate the stations en route to Crosshaven; the navy helped prepare these adornments, and a large building was made available for the ceremonial reception and banquet which would follow the actual opening.

The day's festivities commenced at Cork Albert Street station where, in the morning, the Lord Lieutenant was welcomed by a guard of honour and the Gordon Highlanders Pipe Band, together with 50 members of the Royal Irish Constabulary under County Inspector Rogers and District Inspector Moriarty. The flag-bedecked 'first train' left Cork at 11.30 am, and with Lord Dudley and the other official guests safely aboard, the triumphant journey to Crosshaven began. At Passage, a number of boys from the Industrial School were present, while at Monkstown a party of cadets from the training ship HMS Emerald formed another guard of honour.

Immense crowds awaited the train at Crosshaven, where addresses of welcome were read by the Very Reverend Canon Carey, and also by William Moore Hodder, DL, on behalf of the local Justices of the Peace. In reply, Lord Dudley commented on the great attractions of Crosshaven as a tourist and health resort, and he wished the Cork Blackrock & Passage Railway every success for the future.

Thus, after countless vicissitudes and tribulations, the Crosshaven line was finally opened for public traffic. However, the project had cost no less than £200,093 11s. 11d. The contractor finally received £138,158 17s. 7d., while a further £61,934 14s. 4d. was paid to 'other persons'. The original contract with John Best had been worth £82,040, for which he was to supply creosoted wooden sleepers and undertake all other work, the CB & PR company being responsible for furnishing the rails and other permanent way materials. Following the suspension of the works in 1900 a new contract had, of necessity, been made with Mr Best – though it should perhaps be pointed out that the contractor agreed to accept a large amount of debenture stock in part-payment for the work, and in this way the Best family became substantial holders of 1901 CB & PR debenture stock.

The completed extension line ran southwards from Passage, where the new single line platform had been constructed to the south-east of the original terminus. Continuing due south, the line passed through Passage Tunnel and, following a relatively level course, the route proceeded via Glenbrook and Monkstown. Beyond, the new railway curved south-westwards to reach Raffeen and Carrigaline, and finally turned east-south-east for the approach to Crosshaven. Intermediate stations were provided at Glenbrook, Monkstown, Raffeen and Carrigaline, and the works included a twin span girder bridge over the Owenboy River near Carrigaline, and the 4-span viaduct at Crosshaven.

Narrow Gauge Motive Power

The four 3 ft gauge locomotives ordered from Neilson & Company were of interest in that they had the largest driving wheels of any Irish narrow gauge engines. They were (in comparison to the picturesque antiques that had worked the CB & PR in broad gauge days) both powerful and modern. Their principal dimensions were as follows:

Cylinders (outside)	14.5 in. × 22 in.
Driving wheels	4 ft 6 in. diameter
Leading wheels	3 ft diameter
Trailing wheels	3 ft diameter
Heating surface	801 square feet
Firebox	6 ft 9 in. long
Water capacity	1,200 gallons
Coal capacity	2.5 tons
Boiler pressure	160 lb. per square inch
Weight	37 tons 3 cwt
Coupled wheelbase	8 ft
Total wheelbase	21 ft

The maker's numbers were 5561, 5562, 5563 and 5564.

Externally, the new engines had a sleek, workmanlike appearance, though when seen from the front they had a curiously 'top-heavy' look (an impression reinforced by their unusual buffer beams, which were cut away at each side to give easy access to the cylinders – the resulting shape being roughly triangular). The Neilson locos were numbered in sequence from 4 to 7, the numbers being carried on small plates affixed to the centre of the side tanks, and also in painted numerals on the buffer beams.

Some Other Details

In its narrow gauge guise the CB & PR was both a passenger and goods line, and in addition to its new fleet of 3 ft gauge bogie coaches the company acquired a number of open wagons, vans and cattle wagons.

Railway Constructor

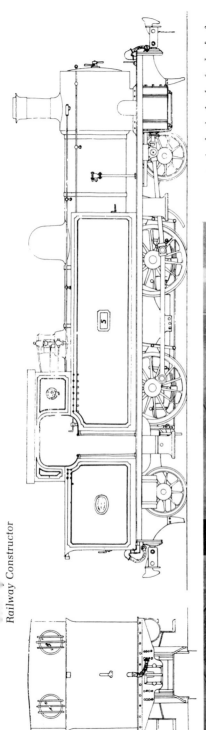

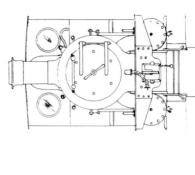

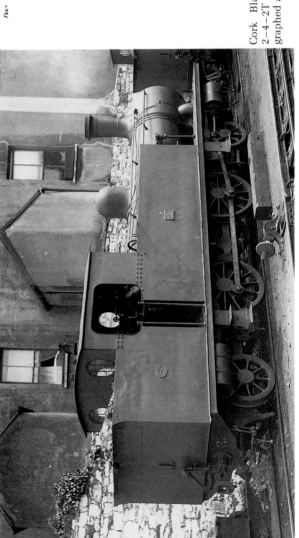

Cork Blackrock & Passage Railway 2–4–2T locomotive No. 5, photographed at Cork on 10th June, 1932.

H.C. Casserley

The ordinary coaches had 6 compartments, but there were also some saloon-brake vehicles with large plate glass windows through which travellers could view the riverside scenery. Each coach was about 36 ft long, the weight being around 12 tons. There were, in all, 12 first class coaches and 16 third class vehicles, the latter having un-upholstered cane seats.

In the Edwardian period, passenger trains seem to have run in rakes of 4–6 vehicles, the usual practice being for one of the distinctive 'saloon brakes' to be marshalled at the rear while (in a six-coach train) another would be positioned in the centre.

H. Fayle, who knew the Cork Blackrock & Passage line in the early 1900s, mentioned that the company's carriage fleet included both first and third class saloon vehicles 'with large plate glass windows at the sides and ends'; one of these coaches was 'usually placed at the rear of the train' so that travellers could view the passing riverside scenery.[4] A typical 6-coach formation would probably have been marshalled as follows: locomotive; 2 third class coaches; 1 saloon brake-first; 2 thirds; 1 saloon brake first.

The CB&PR's heraldic crest was displayed on each coach, together with the company's initials in small letters; the words 'third' or 'first' appeared in full on each door. All of the stock, both passenger and freight, had centrally-placed buffer/couplers. Fayle considered that the passenger rolling stock was 'remarkably good' – although this was only to be expected on a line that relied for its existence on tourism and commuter traffic. Several of the CB&PR coaches were later equipped with coal-gas lighting, the necessary illuminant being supplied by the Cork Gas Company.

The newly-laid 3 ft gauge trackwork consisted of 30 ft steel rails, each rail being sole-plated and fang-bolted to timber sleepers. There were 11 sleepers to each 30 ft length of track and the ballast was formed of broken stone. The rails weighed 68½ lb. per linear yard.

The line was fully signalled, and left-hand running was adhered to on the double track section between Cork and Blackrock, and at stations with intermediate crossing loops. Preece's double line block system was employed between Cork and Blackrock, the remaining sections being worked by Webb-Thompson electric train staff apparatus.

The single track sections between Blackrock and Crosshaven were divided into several staff sections; from 1906 onwards the sections were Blackrock –Rochestown, Rochestown–Passage, Passage–Monkstown, Monkstown–Carrigaline and Carrigaline–Crosshaven.

The main crossing stations for passenger trains were Monkstown and Carrigaline, the loop at Passage being unsuitable for passenger working because it was outside the limits of the passenger platform; an additional crossing loop was installed at Rochestown in 1906.

The Edwardian Period

The ordinary weekday train service provided a basic distribution of eight or nine trains in each direction between Cork and Crosshaven, with an additional three or four short distance workings between Cork and Monkstown. In February 1905 it was announced that a half hourly service would run to and from Crosshaven on summer Sundays; these Sunday trains left Cork Albert Street between 9.30 am and 12 noon, returning from Crosshaven from 7 pm onwards (this would involve the use of at least three of the four engines, leaving little in reserve in the event of a failure). Otherwise the service would be on a regular hourly basis. It was also intended to prolong the season by introducing the summer service in April, instead of June.

As a result of very crowded conditions at certain times during the previous summer a shareholder inquired if extra rolling stock would be obtained, but the Chairman replied that the company was unable to do this; nevertheless, extra trains would run in lieu. (The company had, of course, acquired additional rolling stock for working the extension.) River excursions by steamer from Cork had proved so popular that it was intended to continue them, while it was hoped to improve the existing arrangements between the CB&PR and the Great Southern & Western Railway respecting excursion traffic at Cork and Queenstown.

By August, receipts had increased by £975, 12,279 more passengers having been carried and 8,765 more train miles worked; yet expenses had fallen by £560. Interest on the 1902 debenture stock, which had been in arrears, had since been paid up to 31st December, 1904; earlier, the 1896 interest had also been in arrears but thanks to the assistance of the Governor and Board of the Bank of Ireland the sum due (£4,256) had also been cleared off. Concerning improved receipts, the following comparative figures were furnished:

	1900–1	1904–5
Gross Receipts:	£18,358	£23,341
Working expenses:	£14,900	£14,382
Net profit:	£3,405	£8,859

The re-gauged and extended Cork Blackrock & Passage line was, in many ways, an anomaly. As we have seen, the railway had been built under an Act of Parliament, and in this respect it was a 'main line' in miniature rather than a light railway. The raised platforms, heavy engineering, and of course the Cork to Blackrock double track section were all unusual features on a 3 ft gauge route, but above all, the intensive passenger service provided on this Cork suburban line put the CB&PR into a class of its own.

The additional passing loop installed at Rochestown in 1906 enabled the CB&PR to offer an even better service to the public, and the normal 50 minute journey time for ordinary trains was reduced to 40 minutes. It should also be mentioned that, in summer time, the company operated up and down business expresses which left Crosshaven at 9 am and returned from Cork at 5.35 pm (2 pm on Saturdays); these special fast workings stopped only at Carrigaline. The up train accomplished its journey in 36 minutes, while the corresponding down service reached Crosshaven in only 35 minutes – this was, needless to say, very smart working when the number of obligatory slacks for sharp curves are taken into consideration. In addition, an up express departed from Crosshaven at 7.00 pm on Sunday evenings, calling only at Monkstown.

THROUGH BOOKINGS OF PARCELS BETWEEN GREAT WESTERN STATIONS AND STATIONS IN IRELAND.

Parcels may be booked through at the Railway Clearing House Scale, as per Regulations, to and from all Stations on the Great Western Railway (exclusive of the Channel Islands) and the undermentioned Stations in Ireland via the routes shown (except as shown below).

Exceptions.—The Owner's Risk Scale of rates is not applicable (except so far as Butter is concerned) from or to Great Western Railway Stations West of Bristol and South of the Main Line which runs from London to Bristol, and also from or to the Channel Islands and Irish Interior Stations.

NOTE.—The full addresses of Consignees must in all cases be shown upon Waybills of Parcels booked to Ireland.

CORK, BLACKROCK AND PASSAGE RAILWAY.

Aghada	Haulbowline	Raffeen
Blackrock (Co. Cork)	Monkstown (Co. Cork)	Ringaskiddy
Carrigaline	Passage	Rochestown
Crosshaven	†Queenstown	Spike Island
Glenbrook		

Route viâ Fishguard, Rosslare, Mallow and Cork, or viâ Fishguard, or Bristol, and City of Cork Steam Packet Company.

Steamers sail between Fishguard and Rosslare **twice daily** in both directions.

Steamers leave Fishguard for Cork, **Tuesdays, Thursdays and Saturdays only.**

Steamers leave Bristol on **Thursdays only.**

NOTE.—When Traffic is sent viâ Fishguard and the City of Cork Steam Packet Company on Tuesdays, Thursdays and Saturdays, care must be taken to see that it arrives at Fishguard in time to go forward by the 11.30 p.m. Boat from there on those days.

† Book to Great Southern and Western Company unless specially consigned to Cork, Blackrock and Passage Co.

An extract from a GWR publication entitled *Instructions Relating to Irish Traffic* (1910). Note that the CB & PR Company's steamer piers were regarded as 'stations' for through booking purposes between the GWR and CB & PR systems. *S.C. Jenkins*

In an attempt to attract even more passenger traffic, the company opened a simple halt at Hoddersfield, the residence of William Moore Hodder JP – who not only permitted its erection on his land, but also opened his demesne to school and excursion parties, which was much appreciated. This halt was one mile west of Crosshaven, but is thought to have had a very brief existence, some local residents being unable to recollect its existence, or trains calling there. A similar halt had been opened three years earlier at Ballinure, to the south of Blackrock, beyond two over-bridges, to serve an adjacent coursing venue, the lineside platform comprising a cinder 'mound'.

February 1909 saw £1,400 lodged to the fund for renewal of the locomotives, permanent way, and steamers, the creation of such a fund being considered imperative. The upkeep of the steamer fleet was still very heavy despite every effort to reduce the mileage operated, and it was intended, during the forthcoming summer, to eliminate all uneconomic workings. During the past season a direct service had operated between Queenstown and Crosshaven but with very unsatisfactory results – while the time was not far distant when at least one vessel would have to be replaced.

During the final half-year of 1909 the *Monkstown* (of 1882) had been sold and another paddle vessel, the *Audrey* hired in replacement. The latter had been a popular pleasure steamer on the River Tyne, having a large passenger capacity, also electric light, steam heating, and other modern features. It was stated that the *Monkstown*'s engines were old-fashioned, and wasteful of coal. By August, the company had a second paddle steamer, the *Mabel* on hire from the same source; she was smaller than the *Audrey*, burning 56 lb. of coal per mile, whereas the latter, having heavy engines and greater driving power consumed 109 lb. to the mile.

In the exceptionally wet summer of 1912 the hired paddle steamer *Audrey* was on charter work in Dublin (having been at Weymouth the previous year) and it was understood that she had been very popular with trippers. In view of her absence, tours of Cork Harbour from St Patrick's Bridge in summer had been discontinued.

In general, the Cork Blackrock & Passage steamers ran at a loss as a result of high working costs and the relatively small numbers of passengers using them. Nevertheless, these vessels contributed to overall CB&PR profits insofar as they effectively extended the route to Aghada – the normal practice being for the steamers to run to and from Monkstown, calling intermediately at Ringaskiddy, Haulbowline and Queenstown. This service was maintained throughout the year, whereas Crosshaven was served by summer-only sailings. It should be stressed that the seasonal Cork to Crosshaven steamer service complemented the railway rather than competed with it; it was, for example, possible for tourists to travel outwards to Crosshaven by train and return to Cork aboard a steamer, while a variety of alternative rail-steamer tours were possible via either Crosshaven or Monkstown.

A Vice-Regal Commission

Victorian and Edwardian political thinking favoured free market economic solutions that did not interfere with the freedom of action enjoyed by commercial undertakings. It comes as a surprise, therefore, to discover the ways in which government policies impinged upon the railway industry in England – and to an even greater extent in Ireland. The Irish lines attracted an inordinate amount of official attention throughout the 19th century, and this trend continued into the Edwardian period, with the setting up of a Viceregal Commission to examine the workings of the Irish railway companies. The Commission started taking evidence in October 1906, and in the ensuing months the CB & PR and other Irish lines were most carefully scrutinised.

At length, the Commissioners issued detailed reports on all of the lines concerned. In the case of the Cork Blackrock & Passage Railway they recommended two courses of action whereby the company might improve its financial position by redeeming debenture stock. First, it was suggested that the £65,000 Board of Works loan made in 1901 might be increased by £95,000 at a much reduced rate of interest, and second, the Commissioners recommended a reduction of interest on the original loan. Unfortunately, the Commissioners' financial recommendations were not always implemented, and in any case, World War I intervened before the suggested re-organisation of capital could take place.

Notes

1 PRO file MT6 1311/3.
2 *Ibid.*
3 Being a ceremonial post the office of Lord-Lieutenant was above politics, and individual Lord-Lieutenants were often highly-regarded – even by Home Rulers.
4 H. Fayle, The Cork Blackrock & Passage Railway, *Railway Magazine*, 1909.

Locomotive No. 7 waits in the platform at Albert Street, Cork around 1932.

A.T. Newham

A panoramic view of Passage, showing the railway running through the street to reach Passage Tunnel. The original terminus can be glimpsed in the background.

A.T. Newham

Locomotive No. 4 receives attention at Cork Albert Street. This view provides a rare glimpse of the single road engine shed.   *LCGB, Ken Nunn Collection*

An impressive, broadside view of engine No. 7 at Cork on 15th September, 1929.
H.C. Casserley

CB & PR 2–4–2T locomotive No. 7 waits at Cork Albert Street on 10th June, 1932. Mr Casserley's photograph clearly shows the roof trusses of the train shed.

H.C. Casserley

Locomotive No. 6 stands in Albert Street station during the final years of operation. The first vehicle behind the engine is a third class open with just two doors on each side, while the following coach is an ordinary, 6-compartment third. *A.T. Newham*

Engine No. 4 stands in the bay platform at Cork on 15th September, 1929.

H.C. Casserley

CB&PR 2–4–2T No. 5 stands in the platforms at Cork Albert Street with a mixed freight; covered vans, opens, and two types of cattle wagon can be clearly seen.

LCGB, Ken Nunn Collection

Chapter Four
The Route Described

Having described the history of the Cork Blackrock & Passage Railway, it would now be appropriate to examine the route of the line in greater detail, and the following chapter will take readers on a guided tour of the railway as it would have appeared in narrow gauge days.

Cork Albert Street

Cork Albert Street was a typical suburban station, with lavish passenger facilities but only minimal provision for goods traffic. It was, by narrow gauge standards, a relatively complex terminus, three terminal platforms being available for passenger trains. There was one side platform and one island, the latter having tracks on either side; the outer face of the island platform was equipped with an engine release road which also served as a goods headshunt/siding, while a crossover between the main platforms allowed incoming engines to run-round their trains.

The three platforms were signalled for two-way working, a 3-arm home signal being provided so that trains arriving from Blackrock could enter any of the three platform roads. In the reverse direction, the three platforms each had its own starting signal, and this meant that outgoing trains could depart from either the main platforms or the adjacent bay.

Goods facilities consisted of two sidings on the north side of the running lines which were entered via the above-mentioned engine release road; the sidings were linked at each end to form a loop, and there was an additional crossover roughly half way down the yard. Loading facilities were concentrated on a raised loading dock that flanked one of the two goods sidings.

Other features of interest at Cork Albert Street included a single road locomotive shed, a wooden signal cabin with decorative barge boards, and a large train shed that spanned all four terminal roads and was supported by lightweight metal trusses. A water column allowed locomotives to replenish their tanks, and a pedestrian footbridge extended from north to south across the entire width of the goods yard and running lines.

The main station building (which also contained the CB&PR company offices) was situated at the western end of the train shed. A two-storey, hip-roofed building, it featured arched, Italianate door and window openings on the ground floor, the upper floor windows being rectangular. The building was on a different alignment to that of the train shed, and for this reason a single storey linking structure was provided which physically united the two halves of the station. Like the main building, this single storey wing exhibited Italianate architectural details; its main facade curved through an angle of approximately 40 degrees in order to effect the desired 'join' between the station building and train shed (see accompanying photograph).

The CB&PR station was sited within close proximity to the Cork & Bandon terminus, and in this context it is interesting to note that in 1912, the 'Cork City Railway' was opened as a means of linking the hitherto-isolated Cork & Bandon system to the GS&WR main line at Glanmire Road. Such a link had not been envisaged when the Cork Blackrock & Passage Directors

A detailed view of Cork Albert Street station exterior on 9th July, 1934 – two years after the closure of the CB & PR line. *H.C. Casserley*

A post-closure view of Cork Albert Street, showing the main administrative buildings (*left*) and part of the extensive train shed (*right*). *A.T. Newham*

had taken the decision to convert their own line to 3 ft gauge, and in retrospect, one feels that the CB&PR would not have been narrowed if the Cork City line had been opened back in the 1890s. (Interestingly, the Cork City Railway was in effect a detached portion of the Great Western Railway – most of its capital and three of its four Directors having emanated from Paddington!)

On the subject of Cork connecting lines, one might also recall that, in the 1890s, the proprietors of the Cork & Muskerry Railway had tentatively suggested a scheme whereby their own line could have been linked to the CB&PR via a street tramway. This ambitious proposal had resulted in discussions being held between the two railway companies and the Cork Tramways & Lighting Company, and at one stage the tramway Directors agreed that their line might be altered to a gauge of 2 ft 11½ in. so that ordinary railway vehicles could traverse their system. In the event, this interesting scheme was abandoned, and the CB&PR never became part of a much larger County Cork narrow gauge network (if implemented, this scheme would have resulted in the creation of an extensive 3 ft gauge system, comparable to the County Donegal or other narrow gauge lines in the North of Ireland).

Blackrock

Leaving Cork Albert Street, trains skirted Cork Park Racecourse, and then ran for some distance beside the 'Marina' – an attractive riverside boulevard providing many tantalising views of the River Lee. Running due east on an impressive section of double track, trains followed the river for about one mile, and then turned south-eastwards. Entering the deep cutting near Dundanion Castle the route climbed on a succession of rising gradients, the steepest of which was a short stretch of 1 in 134.

Blackrock, the first intermediate stop, was a little over two miles from Albert Street. Situated in a cutting, the station served a popular riverside resort which was at its peak during the early 1900s. 'The principal object of interest', remarked H. Fayle, was the nearby castle; it was about half a mile from the railway, and occupied 'a commanding position situation at a bend in the river, just where the shores on either side sweep away and form the large sheet of water known as Lough Mahon'.

In operational terms, Blackrock was of some importance in that it marked the end of the double track section from Cork, the junction between double and single track being at the Crosshaven end of the station. Up and down platforms were provided, and there was a footbridge at the north end of the platforms; the main station buildings were on the down (i.e. southbound) side of the line. Other facilities included a wooden 'contractor's' style signal cabin at the south end of the down platform, and a short dead-end spur on the up side.

The station buildings were arranged on two levels – the booking office being at the top of a sloping ramp connecting the platforms with an adjacent road bridge. There were, in addition, some platform-level buildings providing waiting room and other facilities.

A general view of Cork Albert Street, again photographed in GSR days. Items of interest include the water column and the substantial signal box.

Locomotive and General Photographs

The scene at Albert Street on 4th July, 1934, during demolition of the CB&PR line. Scrapped coaches occupy the goods platform, and some of the trackwork has already been lifted.

H.C. Casserley

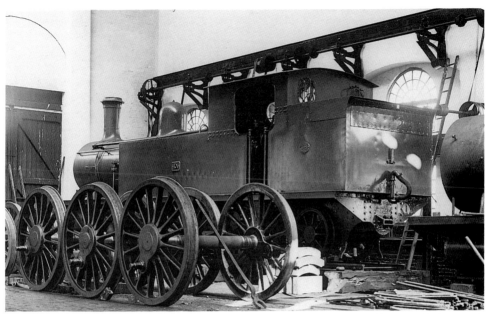

CB&PR 2–4–2T No. 4 in the former Great Southern & Western shops at Cork Glanmire Road on 9th July, 1934. *H.C. Casserley*

Sister engine No. 5 at Glanmire Road on 9th July, 1934. The engines were subsequently transferred to the Cavan & Leitrim section of the GSR. *H.C. Casserley*

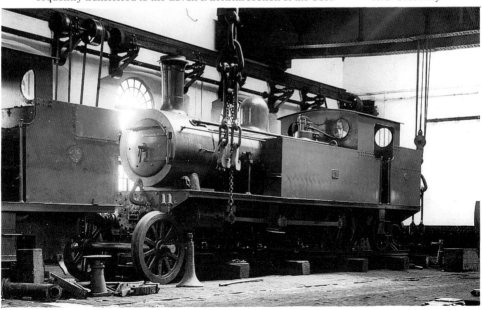

A CB&PR train hurries eastwards along the double track section between Cork and Blackrock; conventional left-hand running was adhered to on this unique section of Irish 3 ft gauge double track. *LCGB, Ken Nunn Collection*

Engine No. 5 at Cork Albert Street in Great Southern days. Note the bell mounted atop the cab roof (necessary because, at Passage, the Crosshaven extension ran through the streets). *Oakwood Collection*

A CB&PR mixed train heads east along the double track beside the River Lee. The formation appears to consist of 1 covered van, 1 goods brake van, 4 open wagons, 2 third class vehicles, a brake first, and finally, 2 more compartment thirds.

W. McGrath Collection

A useful view of the rarely-photographed eastern end of Albert Street station, showing the goods sidings to the left of the main up and down running line.

H.C. Casserley

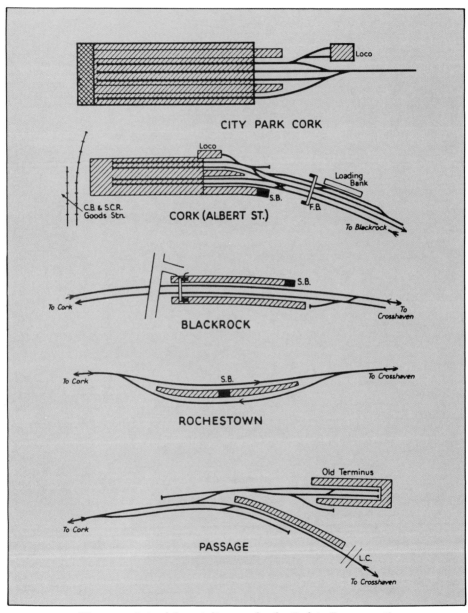

Diagrammatic track layout diagrams for the Cork to Passage section.

Blackrock station in Edwardian days looking towards Cork, and showing the signal cabin to advantage; the footbridge and station buildings can be glimpsed in the background.   *Irish Railway Record Society*

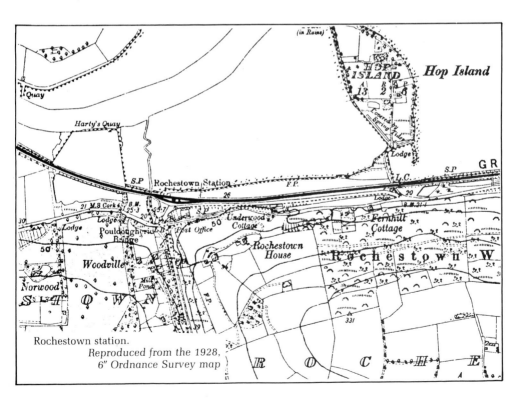

Rochestown station.
*Reproduced from the 1928,
6" Ordnance Survey map*

Rochestown

From Blackrock, the line continued south-eastwards and, after a brief ascent, down trains surmounted a miniature 'summit' before descending towards the Douglas River. The railway was carried across the estuary on a large viaduct composed of horizontal girders resting on masonry piers; always a troublesome structure, the Douglas viaduct was later to prove a tempting target for IRA terrorists (see *Chapter Five*).

Having crossed the Douglas, trains entered Rochestown station, where the track layout consisted of a simple loop. Until 1906 it had been a single-platform stopping place, but improvements carried out in that year transformed Rochestown into a passing station with a centrally-placed island platform between the up and down running lines.

Passage

Running due east beside the wide expanse of water known as Lough Mahon, trains followed a level course as far as Passage. Here, the line had originally ended in a two-platform riverside terminus, with convenient access to and from the adjacent steamer pier. When the Crosshaven extension was built, the layout was altered to provide an entirely new 405 ft-long through platform to the south-east of the original, the revised layout resembling that at Mullingar on the Midland Great Western line, or Dorchester on the London & South Western Railway.

There was originally a short siding to the west of the station, but this was subsequently realigned and extended to form a lengthy running loop. The station building provided in connection with the Crosshaven extension was a semi-prefabricated design incorporating the usual booking office and waiting rooms. The corrugated iron roof swept down in front of the centrally-placed waiting room to form a simple canopy, and an array of stove pipe chimneys projected skywards in true 'Emmett' fashion!

The through platform was built on a noticeable curve, and having left the station trains passed through a gate and into the main street, crossing the latter obliquely and then traversing Back Street. As this crossing was too wide for conventional level crossing gates the four engines were equipped with warning bells for the benefit of careless pedestrians. (The bells were mounted on top of the cab roofs, and can be discerned in most photographs.)

Glenbrook

After running through the street for a distance of about 75 yards, the single line passed beneath a small footbridge and immediately entered the 535 yds-long Passage tunnel. The tunnel mouth was faced with stonework and the top of the arch was formed of brick, though the side walls were made of concrete.

Emerging into daylight once more, trains entered Glenbrook station. This small, single platform station, was 6¾ miles from Cork; it was situated on the foreshore, and featured a gated level crossing. Beyond, the line continued along the foreshore, and as there was very little space between the

Passage station in 1912. Note the corrugated iron station buildings, which were similar to others erected on the Crosshaven extension line.   *W. McGrath Collection*

Passage station, looking north along the through platform (added 1902). The gate in the foreground marked the start of the 'street-section' through Passage. The hut visible to the left of the siding was used by local coal merchants.   *A.T. Newham*

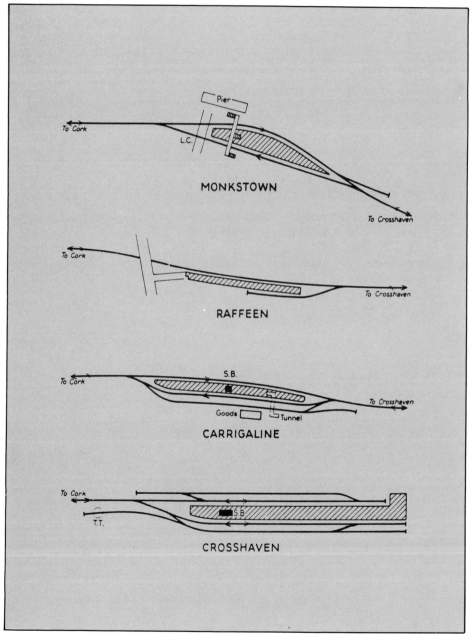

Diagrammatic track layout diagrams for the Crosshaven extension line.

main road and the river bank, it had been necessary to build a concrete embankment when the extension line was constructed. This structure was difficult to maintain and it was, at one stage, extensively rebuilt. In view of the sharp curves on this section, the speed of trains was restricted to 15 mph in a number of places.

As their trains glided southwards along the water's edge travellers could, by glancing eastwards, see the corresponding foreshore of Great Island on the opposite side of the narrow estuary. The rival GS & WR route to Queenstown occupied a similar waterside position on the Great Island shore, but of greater interest (perhaps) to the inquisitive tourist was the little churchyard of Clonmel in which were buried the victims of the torpedoed RMS *Lusitania*. This same churchyard (just ¾ mile north of Queenstown) also contained the grave of the Rev Charles Wolfe (1791–1823), who had composed *The Burial of Sir John Moore*. A short distance north of Monkstown the line passed the once-renowned Glenbrook Baths.

Monkstown

Monkstown, the next stop, was only a short distance further on. A passing place, Monkstown was the outer end of the train staff section from Passage. Another waterside station, its simple track layout consisted of a crossing loop with a centrally-placed island platform and a short dead-end siding at the southern end. Access to the platform was by means of an intricate footbridge that continued eastwards across the down running line to reach the neighbouring steamer pier. The station was controlled from a wooden signal cabin on the up side, and a gated level crossing at the north end of the station enabled road vehicles to reach the steamer pier.

Monkstown was 7¾ miles from Cork and about the same distance from Crosshaven, and being equidistant from both termini it was the usual passing place for up and down services. The station was also an important interchange between rail and river services, and passengers travelling to or from Queenstown via the CB & PR route generally embarked or disembarked here.

Raffeen

Leaving Monkstown, the bustling 2–4–2Ts and their trains of panelled coaches followed the estuary south-westwards to the wayside station of Raffeen. One of the smaller intermediate stopping places *en route* to Crosshaven, Raffeen had just one platform and a short siding for occasional goods traffic; the station served the nearby village of Shanbally, on the south side of the railway.

Carrigaline

From Raffeen, the single line ran south-westwards across the neck of a narrow peninsula. Since Cork, the route had been more or less dead level, but, having left the estuary, down trains were faced with a rising gradient of 1 in 132.

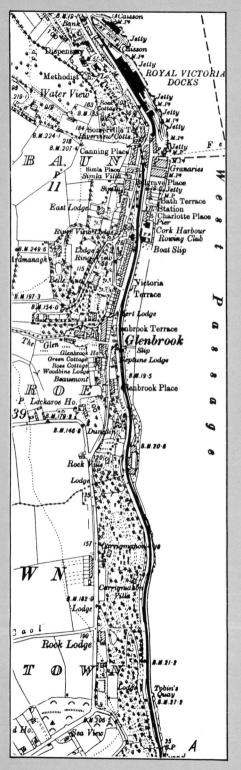

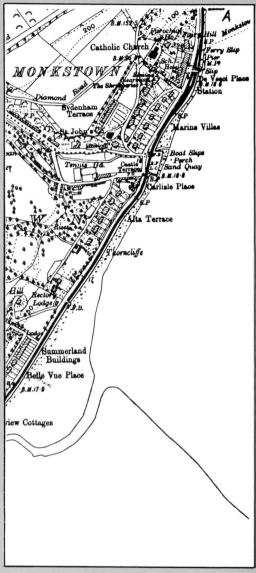

This map shows the railway from Passage to Monkestown.

Reproduced from the 1934, 6″ Ordnance Survey map

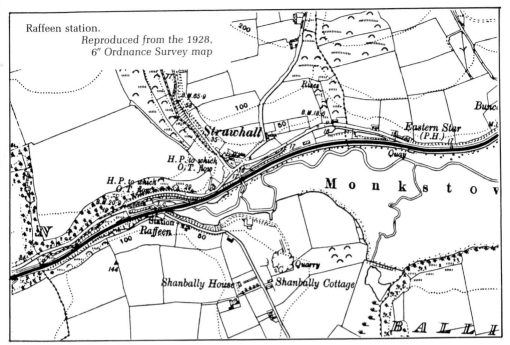

Raffeen station.
Reproduced from the 1928,
6" Ordnance Survey map

Monkstown station from the south, showing the short dead end siding that diverged
from the crossing loop.   *National Library of Ireland*

An interesting Edwardian view of Carrigaline station, showing the contractor's style signal box; coach No. 20, a 3rd class vehicle, can be seen to the left, with a brake first beyond.

National Library of Ireland

RAILWAY STATION, CARRIGALINE, CO.CORK. 9519. W.L.

Carrigaline station, looking north from the station approach road. Note the CB & PR cattle wagon, with its slatted sides and the prominent subway (an unusual feature on a narrow gauge line).

National Library of Ireland

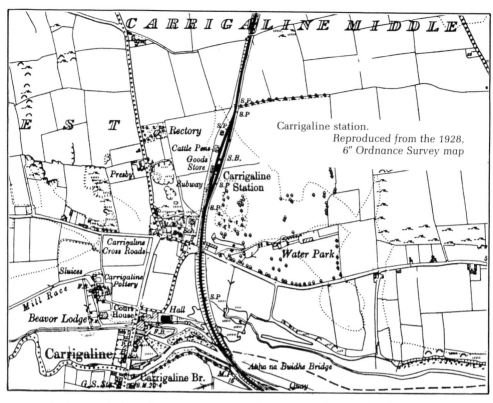

Carrigaline station.
Reproduced from the 1928,
6" Ordnance Survey map

A view south from the same position as the previous photograph. The small hut visible to the left was a ticket office for road services. *National Library of Ireland*

After half a mile, the climb steepened to 1 in 80 as the railway traversed a picturesque valley. Soon, the gradient eased to 1 in 528, and beyond this the route dropped towards Carrigaline on a 1 in 80 falling gradient. Curving gradually southwards, the line then entered the Owenboy Valley, and Carrigaline (11¼ miles) was only a short distance further on.

Carrigaline was, by CB & PR standards an important station, its status being underlined by the presence of a subway connection to and from the island platform! The track plan incorporated two long loops which, between them, provided three parallel lines, that on the west side of the station being for goods traffic. There was, in addition, a short siding at the south end of the goods loop, though the goods shed was located beside the 'main' goods line.

In architectural terms, Carrigaline was similar to the other stations on the 1903 extension line. Its station buildings were like those found elsewhere on the route, one small refinement being an entrance in the south wall through which travellers entered the building after emerging from the subway.

The adjacent signal box was a 1½-storey timber structure which, like those at other CB & PR stations had clearly been erected by specialised signalling contractors. At least some signalling work on the Cork Blackrock & Passage line had been undertaken by Messrs Evans O'Donnell & Co., but interestingly, the signal cabin at Carrigaline was apparently of Railway Signal Co. (or Gloucester Wagon Co.) design; its distinguishing features included large operating floor windows that extended down to floor level, ornate barge boards and finials, and tiny, rectangular windows located high in the wooden gables.

The only other large building at Carrigaline was the arc-roofed goods shed on its raised loading platform. It was built of corrugated iron, and featured sliding doors on each side through which goods could be transhipped between road and rail vehicles. The presence of this shed underlined the fact that Carrigaline was one of the few CB & PR stations to handle goods traffic on a regular basis.

The platform was illuminated by oil lamps placed in tapering glass lanterns, and minor details included the usual assortment of platform furniture – including slender, park-type station seats and at least one large nameboard bearing the name CARRIGALINE in raised letters.

Crosshaven

After Carrigaline, the line followed the Owenboy river eastwards to its destination, but before reaching the south bank trains crossed the river on the two-span Owenboy Bridge. Having gained the south side of the estuary, the route continued parallel to the water – albeit at some distance from the shore.

Once past Carrigaline the estuary broadened to form an attractive well-wooded creek; the combination of woods, water, and an unmistakable Celtic landscape recalled the lush estuaries of the Tamar or Fall, and West Country visitors would doubtless have been pleased to discover that this Cornish-style estuary was known as 'Drake's Pool' in commemoration of Sir Francis Drake (who was said to have sheltered there in 1587).

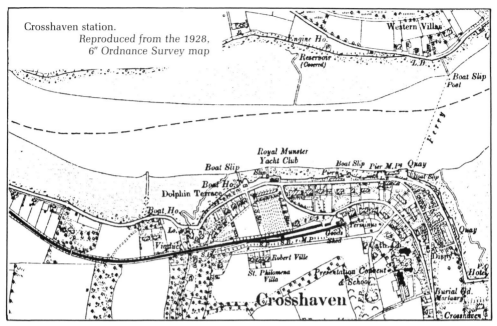

Crosshaven station.
_Reproduced from the 1928,
6" Ordnance Survey map_

At one point between Carrigaline and Crosshaven the winding single line came
within yards of 'Drake's Pool'. _National Museum of Ireland_

CARRIGALINE RIVER.CROSSHAVEN.8840.W.L.

Continuing alongside the estuary for about three miles, down trains climbed sharply and, just before the terminus, they rumbled across a deep wooded ravine on the soaring Crosshaven viaduct. This substantial structure incorporated four lattice girder spans, each of which was 75 ft 6 in. long. These girders rested upon brick piers, the two intermediate ones being 55 ft and 42 ft above local ground level.

Crosshaven station was now in sight, and as trains emerged from the surrounding woods, they had only a short distance to run before they came to a stand beside the 600 ft-long platform at the CB&PR terminus.

Crosshaven had two platform faces, the single platform being, in effect, an island with terminal roads on either side. Both of these dead-end tracks had run-round facilities, and these were also two short spurs at the Cork end of the station – one of which gave access to a turntable. Watering facilities were available for the engines, and there was a small store that was probably used for parcels or 'smalls' traffic sent by passenger train.

The station building was another typical CB&PR structure, its general appearance being similar to the buildings at Passage and Carrigaline. There was a gable-roofed signal box with 24 levers at the opposite end of the platform, and this was, like its counterpart at Carrigaline, a prefabricated design provided by outside contractors.

The two platforms were each signalled for two-way working, twin starters being mounted on a bracket signal at the very end of the platform, while a similar 2-arm assembly enabled incoming trains to enter either platform.

Crosshaven itself was a popular holiday resort during the early 1900s, and the opening of the railway did much to stimulate further resort development in the immediate vicinity. The surrounding area was also of immense strategic importance, and huge forts such as Fort Camden protected this important anchorage. Ship spotters could, in former days, be sure of seeing an interesting assortment of naval and merchant vessels – among them great Atlantic liners such as the *Titanic*, which anchored off Queenstown on 11th April, 1912. A survivor of the sinking (just three days later) recalled how the doomed liner had 'rode up and down on the slight swell in the harbour, a slow, stately dip and recover, only noticeable by watching her bows in comparison with some landmark in the distance'; the approaches to Queenstown had looked 'very beautiful . . . the brilliant morning sun showing up the green hillsides and picking out groups of dwellings dotted here and there above the rugged grey cliffs that fringed the coast'. Three years later, warships and fishing vessels from Queenstown had helped in the rescue of survivors from the torpedoed Cunarder RMS *Lusitania*.

RAILWAY-STATION.CROSSHAVEN.CO.CORK. 8854. W.L.

CROSSHAVEN

A further view of Crosshaven in the early 1900s. Cork Harbour can be seen in the distance, while a 3rd class open coach is prominent in the foreground.

National Library of Ireland

Chapter Five
The Final Years (1912–1932)

The Edwardian era was the heyday of the British and Irish railway system. With the motor car merely a shadow on the horizon, railway companies such as the Great Southern & Western Railway and the Cork Bandon & South Coast held an undisputed monopoly of land transport. It seemed that this monopoly would last for ever – railways were after all, the very symbol of Britain's world-beating industrial technology, and in the early 1900s that technology seemed to have no equals.

The Outbreak of War

Sadly, the halycon Edwardian era was brought to an abrupt and brutal termination on 4th August, 1914, when the German army swept into tiny, defenceless Belgium. In response to this unprovoked attack on a small and inoffensive country, the British government declared war on the aggressors – and the United Kingdom of Great Britain & Ireland thereby became involved in a major European conflict after a century of peace.

Like all railways, the Cork Blackrock & Passage line was immediately touched by the war. Crosshaven station, for example, was closed to civilian traffic just 10 days after the outbreak of hostilities, and this summary action effectively ended all excursion traffic. Summer residents were asked to leave immediately, and police and army sentries were posted at the station and pier – no one being allowed to enter or leave unless they could produce a special permit.

The restriction placed on non-essential passenger traffic was a severe blow to the Cork Blackrock & Passage Railway which, as we have seen, was heavily-biased towards the carriage of tourists. The company was in a serious financial position by 31st December, 1915, and with rumours of closure in the air there were suggestions that the CB & PR line might be sold to the Cork Electric Tramways; indeed, Mr H.H. Nalder, the manager of the tramways, had preliminary talks with the CB & PR Directors in anticipation that the railway could be electrified as part of the tramway system – though in the event this novel proposal was not seriously pursued.

In February 1916 it was reported that, for the first time, interest payments on the Board of Works loan could no longer be met. The reasons for this sad state of affairs were complex; the cessation of tourist traffic to and from Crosshaven was of course a major factor, but in addition the hostilities in Europe contributed to a sharp rise in the cost of coal, rails, uniforms and other materials. The price of coal, for instance, soon rose to 31s. per ton, as opposed to 22s. 4d. per ton prior to 1914. At the same time, the CB & PR had to find an extra £1,650 for the replacement of a timber jetty at Queenstown, while wages and salaries had risen by £974 (with arrears) as a result of wartime inflation.

The unsatisfactory state of Cork Blackrock & Passage finances led to a series of complaints from disgruntled shareholders – among them Messrs Best who had accepted 1901 debenture stock in part-payment of their claims against the company. There were, by 1915, over six years arrears of interest on the 1901 debentures, while the situation regarding ordinary and prefer-ence shares was even worse in that no interest of any kind had been paid since 1899.

At the behest of Messrs Best the Cork Blackrock & Passage Board resolved that a competent railway officer would be brought in to investigate the management of the company, and as a result Mr H.G. Burgess (the Irish Traffic Manager of the London & North Western Railway) was commis-sioned to produce a report on the railway. Perhaps surprisingly, he found that the undertaking was being carefully and economically worked, and every effort had been made to develop all classes of traffic. On the other hand, the report suggested that the conversion of the line to narrow gauge, and its extension to Crosshaven, had cost £24,667 per mile, whereas a line of this nature *should* have cost only £9,000 per mile. Furthermore, Mr Burgess expressed a personal opinion in that the conversion to narrow gauge was thought to have been a mistake – although it was, of course, too late to change this fateful decision.

A reconstruction of the capital was recommended, and the view expressed that the Board of Works – having regard to the value of the line to the surrounding district – would be amenable to some re-arrangement of the £65,000 loan. It was, however, impracticable for the company to meet arrears of interest on the 1901 debentures, and costs and wages were ex-pected to rise still further.

The outbreak of war placed great strains on the Cork Blackrock & Passage steamer fleet, the railway vessels being called upon to carry large quantities of military equipment to Haulbowline and other important establishments in the Cork area. There were five ships in service in 1914; these were the *Rostellan, Queenstown, Albert, Mabel* and *Audrey*. The *Mabel* and *Audrey*, both of which were paddle steamers, were recent acquisitions, having been purchased in 1913. The PS *Audrey* was, however, sold in 1914, and as the remaining vessels were inadequate in relation to the demands of wartime traffic a former Welsh collier, the screw steamer *Taffy* was purchased for the transport of coal supplies from South Wales. Built in 1894, the SS *Taffy* was about 100 ft long, with a beam of 9 ft.

Under Government Control

Railways on mainland Britain had been placed under government control on the outbreak of war, but, for a variety of reasons, the Irish lines were not involved in this emergency measure. Many Irish railwaymen felt that gov-ernment control would result in higher wartime bonuses, and when they threatened strike action over this issue the railways were placed under government supervision under an Order in Council made on 22nd Decem-ber, 1916. This measure came into force on 1st January, 1917, an executive committee consisting of the managers of the five largest Irish lines being set up on behalf of the Board of Trade. As a corollary, the British government agreed to pay compensation to the railway companies, the arrangement being that receipts would be made up to those paid back in 1913.

Happily, Cork Blackrock & Passage receipts soon showed a remarkable increase, the net revenue for 1916 being double that of the previous year.

The Board of Works loan interest up to November was, in consequence, paid, together with a half-year's interest on the 1846 debentures. A claim for government compensation respecting the closure of Crosshaven station had been heard by the Defence of the Realm Losses Commission, but the results so far had been unfavourable to the company.

On 19th November, 1916 the steamer *Taffy* had been lost in a storm off the Welsh coast but, thankfully, no lives were lost; as the vessel and cargo were both fully insured the Cork Blackrock & Passage Railway received £2,970 from the underwriters. (The policy of shipping coal direct to Ireland in CB&PR vessels had been adopted to obviate freight charges.)

In 1918 the CB&PR had a record year for gross receipts, which totalled over £45,000, derived mainly from intensive passenger traffic, but the 50 per cent fares increase imposed by Government orders had considerably helped to swell these figures. Expenditure, however, was also a record at £37,918.

These vastly increased receipts reflected the continued popularity of the CB&PR line, and also its usefulness as a means of transporting large numbers of workmen to and from Passage docks and nearby Haulbowline. Both Passage and Rushbrooke docks had recently been acquired by the shipping firm of Furness Withy, who were actively developing them. Nevertheless, workmen's traffic was unremunerative in view of the very low fares charged, which were similar to pre-war rates, e.g. 2s. 3d. for a 12-journey ticket.

In consequence of the heavy wartime traffic, the Railway Executive transfered five 3rd-class coaches (three from the Londonderry & Lough Swilly Railway) and a locomotive from Northern Ireland. The loco concerned was No. 1 *Alice* of the County Donegal Railways, a 2–4–0T built by Sharp, Stewart (Works No. 3023) in 1881 for the West Donegal line and having the following dimensions:

Cylinders	13 in. × 20 in.
Driving wheels	3 ft 6 in.
Leading wheels	2 ft 6 in.
Heating surface	555 square feet
Grate area	9.75 square feet
Water capacity	500 gallons
Coal capacity	1 ton
Boiler pressure	120 lb. per square inch
Weight	20 tons

Unfortunately, *Alice* could not work beyond Monkstown – possibly because of the heavy gradients – but she enabled the company to provide extra workmen's trains at a critical period. The little engine seems to have been well-liked by CB&PR enginemen, and in the event the 2–4–0T was destined to remain on the Cork line for three years. In 1918, *Alice* ran 7,099 miles on the CB&PR, rising to 16,073 miles in 1919. In the following year she accomplished 3,737 miles, and had become so much a feature of Cork Blackrock & Passage operations that the Directors offered to buy the engine for £400. This offer was not accepted, and the locomotive was eventually returned to County Donegal in 1921.

The 'Troubles' of 1920–23

The Great War ended on 11th November, 1918, but sadly, there was little peace in Ireland. The question of 'Home Rule' had been a bitterly-contested issue for many years, but in 1914 the leaders of the Irish party had committed themselves to the common struggle against Germany. Undeterred by this pledge, the more extreme Irish nationalists staged a sacrificial rising in Dublin in April 1916 – thereby provoking a series of executions that served to enrage the 'nationalist' population of Ireland. By 1920, much of Ireland was in open revolt against the increasingly-unpopular Union with England.

For a time, the Cork Blackrock & Passage Railway continued to operate more or less undisturbed by these momentous events. Traffic to and from Passage Docks was still heavy, and before 1919 workmen's traffic had outgrown even the extra workmen's trains and it became necessary to tell the Passage dock authorities to restrict the number of travel vouchers issued to their employees. It was understood that the Railway Executive had applied to the Board of Trade to remedy the situation but no decision had resulted.

Meanwhile, the company's summer Sunday train service, due to the restrictions imposed, was but a shadow of the past. The wartime restrictions had in fact been relaxed, albeit slightly, in 1915, but only one train was allowed to run – and this was filled to capacity hours before the advertised departure time, thousands of disappointed travellers being left behind at Cork. Following representations a slight increase in Sunday services was later allowed, but severe coal shortages ensured that restrictions on leisure travel remained in force for some time after the end of the war.

The Irish Railway Executive Committee was kept in being until 31st December, 1919, on which date control of the railways passed to the newly-formed Ministry of Transport (the IREC being retained thereafter in an unofficial capacity). Government control nevertheless continued until midnight on 15th August, 1921, by which time the Ministry of Transport had agreed on the level of compensation that would be paid vis-à-vis the wartime years.

Meanwhile, the introduction of an eight-hour working day on the railways in April 1919 had led to an increase of £7,665 in the company's wage bill, and a 25 per cent increase in the number of staff. Gross receipts up to 31st December were £50,340 (which included £11,716 of Government compensation) but expenditure totalled £43,588, leaving a net balance of only £6,752; interest had, however, been paid on the Board of Works loan and on all debenture stocks other than the 1901 issue. Conversely, goods traffic was down by £908, having been curtailed in view of the new working hours, its volume not justifying the rostering of double crews to cater for it on the same scale as in the past.

There had been a marked fall in gross receipts (£35,254 compared with £43,327), which was ascribed to a number of causes, among them the termination of steamer services after 15th August, 1921, a big English coal strike (1921), traffic restrictions, the curfew (imposed during the Irish 'Troubles') and the military ban on railway operation during August. The closing down of the steamer services was the result of their operation costing

£15,100 per annum against a revenue of only £7,291 – in other words, the company was spending 42 shillings to earn £1! However, in January it was decided to re-instate a goods service, but an ensuing strike prevented this, although the crews were willing work once new terms had been arranged.

Throughout this period, the situation in Ireland had shown an alarming deterioration. Incensed by the activities of the 'Irish Republican Army', the British military authorities had responded ruthlessly, an ill-disciplined force known colloquilly as 'The Black & Tans' (because of their part-police and part-army uniforms) being used to meet terror with counter terror. In December 1920 the 'Tans' maliciously burned down much of Cork, causing damage estimated at something between £2,000,000 and £3,000,000.

In 1921 a treaty culminated in the creation of 'The Irish Free State' as a self-governing dominion within the British Empire, and 26 Irish counties thereby seceded from the United Kingdom, leaving just six predominantly Protestant counties within the Union. Sadly, the IRA refused to accept 'Home Rule' on these terms, and by 1922 there was renewed civil war between the IRA and the newly-created Free State army.

The year 1922 was, not surprisingly, a disastrous one, not only for the Cork Blackrock & Passage line, but also for many other Southern Irish railways. The extreme republicans had always viewed the railway system as a 'soft' target for sabotage, and while the civil war lasted signal boxes were frequently burnt down, and bridges were destroyed. One of the most spectacular acts of destruction was the blowing-up of the GS & WR's large viaduct at Mallow, which resulted in Cork being completely cut off by rail from Dublin and Waterford. On the Cork Blackrock & Passage Railway, Carrigaline bridge was wrecked (but subsequently repaired) while on August 8th a span of the Douglas viaduct was blown up, collapsing into the estuary, and bringing rail services to a complete standstill for eight months. Free State troops had recently landed at Passage (to march on Cork, which was in the hands of dissident Republicans) and an engagement took place near Rochestown: thus the above act of sabotage was probably intended to fulfil a 'strategic' function at a time when the irregular forces of the IRA were falling back towards their strongholds in the south and west.

On 28th January, 1922, for the first time in the history of the company, the staff went on strike, without previous notice; a number of them also took forcible possession for the major part of two days of Albert Street terminus and refused to allow access by the officials of the railway. This action was, however, condemned by the union concerned. Fortunately the dispute was settled, on the basis of new terms, just before the Annual General Meeting of 28th February, and the Chairman expressed the hope that no recurrence of such action would occur as this would embarrass the new Irish Free State Provisional Government.

Other considerations notwithstanding, the stoppages and disruptions of the civil war years caused unemployment and distress to many loyal members of the company's staff, while the CB & PR Board deplored the inconvenience suffered by their patrons during this difficult period. As a stop-gap measure, the steamer *Hibernia* was hired and, with the paddle steamer *Albert*, a passenger service was instituted between Cork and the various

The triple-span girder bridge across the Douglas River, near Rochestown. This structure was blown up by the IRA in 1922; here, repair work is apparently in progress, lifting equipment being evident on the undamaged central span.

W. McGrath Collection

The bridge was eventually repaired by the newly-formed Free State Army, and this rare 1922 photograph shows the first train to cross the repaired bridge. (Cork's railways suffered severely during the Civil War, and it could be argued that the CB & PR never recovered from these acts of sabotage.) *W. McGrath Collection*

riverside piers. A second goods vessel was also introduced for the convenience of traders, but these were essentially temporary expedients that did
little to alleviate the problems caused by the cessation of rail services.
The Irish Civil War ended in May 1923 – by which time Passage Workshops had been seriously damaged, and a number of coaches burnt to
cinders. The cost of making good all this was very heavy, and far beyond the
company's means; unless Government finance was forthcoming, the line
would perforce remain derelict. On the other hand, before hostilities had
ended a hastily-organised but very efficient Railway Repair and Maintenance Corps was created within the new Irish Army; an early achievement
of this body was the construction of a temporary timber bridge in replacement of the dislodged span of the Douglas viaduct.

By the end of 1923, the Douglas viaduct had been permanently repaired (it
may only have been necessary to lift the fallen end of the dislodged span
from the estuary and replace entire on the piers again), and the signal boxes
at Rochestown, Passage, and Monkstown rebuilt, the Blackrock cabin being
in course of reconstruction by February 1924. Gross receipts for the year had
totalled £29,868 but expenditure was £32,260, making a deficit of £2,492,
largely comprising payments for malicious injuries.

The End of Local Control

The Civil War may have ended, but upheavals of another kind were soon
to engulf the Cork Blackrock & Passage line. In mainland Britain, the
government had decided that the diverse railway companies that had grown
up in Victorian times would be 'grouped' into four large undertakings. This
development was echoed in Southern Ireland, where the newly-created Free
State government decided that, as an alternative to full nationalisation, the
existing railway companies would be grouped into a single concern, to be
known as the Great Southern Railways. The proposed amalgamation scheme
would include all lines within the 26 counties of southern Ireland, though
the Great Northern Railway (Ireland) and other cross-border routes would, of
necessity, be excluded.

A Bill to facilitate the Great Southern Amalgamation scheme was introduced in 1924, and in the meantime the various railway undertakings were
urged to pursue voluntary amalgamation before 31st August. The Great
Southern & Western and Cork Bandon & South Coast companies were amenable to the idea of a merger, and in January 1925 the Railway Magazine
reported that the GS & WR, CB & SCR and Midland Great Western companies
had amalgamated, the arrangements having been approved by the Irish Free
State Railway Tribunal on 12th November, 1924.

Some companies, notably the Dublin & South Eastern Railway (which
favoured a policy of union with the GNRI) resisted forced amalgamation, but
small railways such as the CB & PR were in no position to remain in being as
independent undertakings – although some proprietors may have hoped
that the Passage line could manage to evade Great Southern control.

The future of the Cork Blackrock & Passage line was discussed at a shareholders' meeting held on 13th August, 1924. The forthcoming merger was

the main item on the agenda, but there was little comfort for those still hoping to retain control of the company; the Chairman, Sir Stanley Harrington, remarked that the undertaking had 'never been prosperous enough to put by large reserves for renewals, or help dividends in bad years'. There was little opposition to the proposed amalgamation scheme – such opposition would, in any case, have been pointless – and so the popular Cork to Crosshaven line, which had carried many thousands of tourists to the riverside resorts and across the River Lee, after 74 years, passed into GSR ownership.

Looking back, it is patently obvious that the steamer department, with the inevitable maintainence and renewal of vessels, had proved a financial 'millstone around the company's neck'; better receipts might have been possible if the Board had made a good working agreement with an independent operator, in connection with the company's trains, with through bookings and a reasonable division of receipts on a percentage basis, the operator being responsible for maintenance and replacement costs.

After taking over the railway, the new owners added the prefix 'P' (Passage) to the serial numbers of both motive power, classified 'FN1', and rolling stock. In early Great Southern days a reasonably frequent train service was maintained, but as regards the former CB&PR steamer fleet, the new owners lost no time in bringing the matter of disposing of the surviving vessels, *Queenstown*, *Albert* and *Rostellan* before an Officer's Conference on 23rd January, 1925. Two of the steamers were only certified to carry goods, while the third would lose its certificate on 1st April, 1925.

On 27th February a final meeting of the CB&PR Board was held, and it was reported that 1924 had been the worst year on record, owing to a persistently wet summer, a trade depression,and the dearth of work at Passage and Rushbrooke Docks. A sum of £1,250 from the remaining financial assets was voted to the Directors, who were retiring, and this was virtually the end of the undertaking.

Less than three months later, on 5th May, 1925, a Great Southern committee authorised the General Manager to subsidise a steamer service, up to £5 weekly, between Cobh (Queenstown) and Aghada, a further minute of the 7th indicating that R. Warren Young's motorboat service was to carry parcels and merchandise between the above points. No reference was made to cross-river services, which suggests the adoption of a policy of routing all traffic for Cobh and beyond via the longer Cork–Cobh branch of the former GS&WR. This would seem to be confirmed by the absence from the 1926 timetables of any cross-river services. Nevertheless, during the summer on Sundays, there were through trains to Crosshaven at 11.30 am, 2.50, 3.20 and 7.45 pm, with return workings at 2.00, 3.00, 4.00 and 7.30 pm. In addition, non-stop 'down' services left Cork at 10.50 am, and 8.30 pm, with 'up' workings at 11.40 am, 1.10 and 8.30 pm.

The End of The Steamer Fleet

The remaining CB&PR steamers were disposed of at intervals between 1925 and 1927, the first to go being the SS *Queenstown* (II) which was sold

Locomotives Nos. 7, 5 and 6 pose for Mr Casserley's camera at Cork on 10th June, 1932.   *H.C. Casserley*

Locomotive No. 4 departs from Carrigaline with a down train.   *Rex Murphy*

to W. Jones of Lydney, Gloucestershire in July 1925. Next year saw the sale of the SS *Rostellan* to Joseph M'Swiney of Passage, and finally, in 1927, the veteran paddle steamer *Albert* was towed to England for breaking up.

It would perhaps be useful, at this point, to list the last steamers operated by the CB&PR, and the following table will therefore summarise the five vessels purchased or hired by the company during World War I and the years that followed.

Table 4
VESSELS OPERATED BY THE CB&PR 1914–1925

Type	Name	Details
SS	Rostellan	See Table 2.
SS	Queenstown	See Table 2.
PS	Albert	See Table 2.
PS	Mabel	Built Newcastle 1891, length 106 ft, beam 15.7 ft, depth 6.8 ft. New tonnage 57. Hired 1910 and later purchased. She replaced *Monkstown* in 1910, and was originally owned by Mr Harrington, Lee View, Cork.
PS	Audrey	Came to City of Cork Steam Packet Co, 1910. Hired by CB&PRy. Gross tonnage 203. Both this vessel and the *Mabel* were originally River Tyne vessels. Sold 1914. On charter work Weymouth, 1911, Dublin, 1912.
SS	Taffy (collier)	Screw vessel built Port Glasgow, 1894. Length 100.5 ft, beam 21.1 ft, depth 9.3 ft. Net tonnage 73. Lost in storm off Welsh coast on 19th November, 1916.
PS	Empress	Originally built for Goole and Hull Steamship Co. at White-inch, 1893. HP 25, length 140.2 ft, beam 17.1 ft, depth 7.3 ft. Gross tonnage 156. Disposed of by CB&PR in 1922. Obtained 1918, in replacement of *Mabel*.
	Hibernia	Hired 1922 by CB&PR.

Rundown & Closure of the CB&PR

Faced with growing bus and lorry competition, the Great Southern was forced to initiate economies on the former CB&PR route, and in 1927 the double track section between Cork and Blackrock was reduced to single line. Paradoxically, in 1929, the workshops at Passage were moved back to Albert Street, and, in the following year, the overhead gantry was similarly transferred, and a wheel pit was installed at the Cork terminus. These changes and improvements suggested that the GSR intended to retain the CB&PR line – but, sadly, the line was closed completely in 1932.

The timetable provided during these last years was similar to that in operation during the Cork Blackrock & Passage era. In October 1929, for example, local travellers had a choice of six up and six down trains throughout between Cork and Crosshaven. There were, in addition, several short distance workings between Cork and Monkstown, together with a solitary

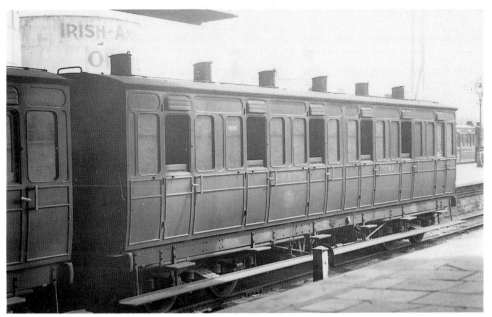

A detailed look at CB&PR coach No. 24 at Cork on 10th June, 1932.

H.C. Casserley

The remains of coach No. 31 after removal of its chassis and bogies. The vehicle appears to have broken its back during removal from Cork, Albert Street.

H.C. Casserley

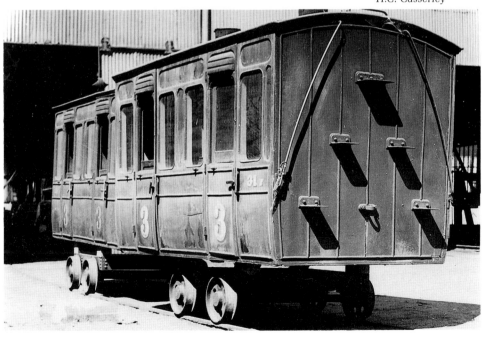

morning up service that started from Carrigaline at 8.00 am. The best down train was the early morning 'express' service from Albert Street which left at 6.05 am and arrived in Crosshaven just 40 minutes later, having called only at Monkstown. Other down services departed from Cork at 7.50, 8.50, 9.50, 11.00 am, 1.15, 3.00, 5.10, 6.15 and 9.15 pm. In the reverse direction, up trains left Crosshaven at 6.50, 8.50, 11.00 am, 1.15, 4.00 and 7.30 pm.

By the early 1930s, the Crosshaven line, and indeed the Great Southern generally had been operating at a loss, due mainly to the effects of road competition and the public giving preferential patronage to the newer form of transport (although by 1928 the GSR had secured a controlling interest in their principal competitor, the Irish Omnibus Company). Inevitably, the end of the Cork Blackrock & Passage line was foreshadowed early in 1932, when it was announced that as a result of continued losses, the Great Southern Directors had reluctantly decided to close it. This resulted in threats, abuse, and the inevitable protest meetings, while early in May a telegram was sent to the Minister of Industry and Commerce urging him to intervene to keep the line open until 31st December, thus affording time for further considera-tion of the matter.

All such efforts were, however, in vain, and on 31st May, 1932 the Monkstown–Crosshaven section was closed. It is a matter of conjecture why this portion of the line was not retained in use until early September, to avail of any summer traffic offering. Finally, on 10th September, the last train ran from Albert Street to Monkstown, and thus after 82 years the Cork Blackrock & Passage Railway passed out of existence, the usual bus services being substituted. (It may be mentioned that in the previous year, the city electric tramway system had been replaced by Irish Omnibus Company double-decked buses.)

The four Cork Blackrock & Passage locomotives were sent away for further service on the Cavan & Leitrim section of the GSR. The engines arrived on the C&L between August and September 1934, the first three having been overhauled at Cork while the fourth was dealt with in the GSR's main workshops at Inchicore. In their new role, they were renumbered from 10L to 13L ('L' standing for Leitrim). Although designed for use on relatively fast suburban trains, the ex-CB&PR locos coped quite well with heavily-laden mineral trains – and C&L section drivers are said to have appreciated their turn of speed. No. 11L was scrapped in 1939, but the remaining engines lasted until the 1950s, No. 13L being scrapped in 1954 while its companions lasted until the end of the C&L in 1959.

About 34 goods vehicles were also sent north to the former Cavan & Leitrim Railway for further service. Many of these were standard CB&PR opens, but others were converted into coal wagons at Inchicore prior to transfer. Two of the transferred goods vehicles were fully-enclosed goods brake vans, and like the ex-CB&PR engines, they remained in service until the 1950s.

The CB&PR coaches were probably sold off locally in Cork, while the CB&PR itself was lifted in 1933–34. Much of the land was sold to Cork County Council, while a school was established in Crosshaven terminus. (At Carrigaline, the station buildings were, for a time, used as a district court-

Carrigaline station, looking towards Crosshaven in September 1968. The station building can be seen to the right, while the neighbouring goods shed is partially hidden by later extensions. *A.T. Newham*

The main street at Passage, through which the CB&PR once ran *en route* to Crosshaven. *A.T. Newham*

Blackrock station, looking towards Cork in September 1968.
A.T. Newham

All trains first and third class.

CORK, PASSAGE, MONKSTOWN, AND CROSSHAVEN.

WEEK DAYS——DOWN.

		a.m	a.m	a.m.	a.m.	a.m.	p.m	p.m	p.m	p.m	p.m			noon			p.m			p.m.	
CORK (Albert St.)	Dep.	6 5	7 50	8 50	9 50	11 0	1 15	3 0	5 10	6 15	9 15	..	..	12 0	..	..	3 0	..	..	5 30	..
Blackrock	,,	..	..	8 55	9 55	11 5	1 20	3 5	5 15	6 20	9 20	..	..	12 5	..	..	3 5	..	..	5 35	..
Rochestown	,,	..	8 0	9 0	10 0	11 10	1 25	3 10	5 20	6 25	9 25	..	..	12 10	..	..	3 10	..	..	5 40	..
Passage	,,	..	8 6	9 6	10 6	11 16	1 31	3 16	5 26	6 31	9 31	..	..	12 16	..	..	3 16	..	..	5 46	..
Glenbrook	,,	..	..	9 10	10 10	11 20	1 35	3 20	5 30	6 35	9 35	..	..	12 20	..	..	3 20	..	..	5 50	..
MONKSTOWN	Arr.	6 25	8 15	9 15	10 15	11 25	1 40	3 25	5 35	6 40	9 40	..	..	12 25	..	..	3 25	..	..	5 55	..
MONKSTOWN	Dep.	6 26	8 16	9 17	..	11 26	..	3 26	..	6 41	..	..	..	12 27	..	..	3 26	..	..	5 56	..
Raffeen (For Shanbally)	,,	..	D	9 23	..	11 32	..	3 32	..	6 47	..	..	..	12 32	..	..	3 32	..	..	6 2	..
Carrigaline	,,	..	8 30	9 30	..	11 40	..	3 40	..	6 55	..	..	..	12 40	..	..	3 40	..	..	6 10	..
CROSSHAVEN	Arr.	6 45	8 40	9 40	..	11 50	..	3 50	..	7 5	..	..	..	12 50	..	..	3 50	..	..	6 20	..

WEEK-DAYS——UP.

		a.m.	a.m.	a.m.	a.m.	a.m.	p.m	p.m	p.m	p.m	p.m.		p.m.		p.m.		p.m.	
CROSSHAVEN	Dep.	6 50	..	8 50	..	11 0	1 15	4 0	..	7 30	..	..	1 0	..	4 10	..	6 30	..
Carrigaline	,,	7 0	8 0	9 0	..	11 10	1 25	4 15	..	7 40	..	..	1 10	..	4 20	...	6 40	..
Raffeen (For Shanbally)	,,	7 8	8 8	9 8	..	11 18	1 33	4 23	..	7 48	..	..	1 18	..	4 28	....	6 48	..
MONKSTOWN	Arr.	7 15	8 15	9 16	..	11 26	1 41	4 31	..	7 56	..	..	1 26	..	4 36	..	6 56	...
MONKSTOWN	Dep.	7 16	8 16	9 17	10 20	11 27	1 42	4 32	5 45	7 57	9 45	..	1 27	..	4 37	..	6 57	...
Glenbrook	,,	7 20	8 21	9 22	10 25	11 32	1 47	4 37	5 50	8 2	9 50	..	1 32	..	4 42	..	7 2	...
Passage	,,	7 26	8 25	9 26	10 29	11 36	1 51	4 41	5 54	8 6	9 54	..	1 36	..	4 46	..	7 6	...
Rochestown	,,	7 31	8 31	9 32	10 35	11 41	1 57	4 47	6 0	8 12	10 0	..	1 42	..	4 52	..	7 12	...
Blackrock	,,	7 36	8 36	9 37	10 40	11 46	2 3	4 52	6 5	8 17	10 5	..	1 47	..	4 57	..	7 17	...
CORK (Albert St.)	Arr.	7 40	8 40	9 42	10 45	11 52	2 7	4 57	6 10	8 22	10 10	..	1 52	..	5 2	..	7 22	...

D—Stops by Signal only.

Passenger timetable for October, 1929.

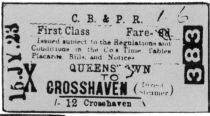

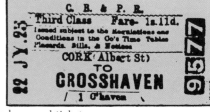

A selection of CB&PR Edmondson card tickets.

house.) At Cork, the former terminus remained derelict for several months, but the site was eventually sold by auction for £4,450 on 29th July, 1936.

Cork Blackrock & Passage Tickets

The study of tickets is a neglected aspect of railway history, and it would therefore be worthwhile to say a few words about the development of CB&PR tickets.

In common with most other railways throughout the world the Cork Blackrock & Passage Railway issued standard Edmondson card tickets. In the early days these were plain cards bearing the names of issuing stations and destinations, together with dates and serial numbers, but by the turn-of-the-century the Cork Blackrock & Passage ticket system had become more complex; the company's initials were displayed on the top of each ticket, and a variety of other information was squeezed onto the tiny cards. The most interesting feature of the CB&PR ticketing system was the way in which the company had evolved a colour code for each type of booking. First class returns, for example, were yellow and white – the 'down' half of the ticket being white while the 'up' half was yellow. A similar situation pertained in the case of third class tickets, the directional colours being, in this case, green and buff. Ordinary singles seem to have followed the same basic directional colours; a first class ticket from Cork to Crosshaven, for instance, would be white, whereas a corresponding ticket for travel in the up direction would have been yellow.

Edmondson card tickets were also used on the company's steamers, and these seem to have followed the same colour-coded system as the railway issues – thus a third class ticket from Agada steamer pier to Cork would be green. Various vertical or horizontal stripes were superimposed to denote through bookings, circular tours or excursions, the resulting tickets being particularly colourful. Some of these interesting specimens have survived in private collections, and although it would take too much space to describe the systems of overprints in detail the following examples will give at least some idea of how the system worked in practice:

Booking	Class	Type	Colour codes
Cork to Crosshaven	1st	single	white
Cork to Crosshaven	1st	return	yellow/white
Cork to Crosshaven	1st	Sunday excursion	yellow/white + red stripe
Queenstown to Crosshaven	1st	steamer	white
Queenstown to Crosshaven	1st	rail/steamer	blue + white stripe
Queenstown to Crosshaven	3rd	rail/steamer	salmon + white stripe
Cork to Crosshaven	1st	excursion	buff
Crosshaven to Cork	3rd	return	green/buff
Monkstown to Cork	1st	single	yellow

The Cork Blackrock & Passage was a commuter line as well as summer tourist route, and it comes as no surprise to find that season tickets were available for travel either by train or steamer service. As a way of fostering regular suburban traffic, the CB&PR followed the example of the Belfast &

Northern Counties, Metropolitan and other enterprising lines by offering 'villa tickets' to the owners or occupiers of any new house built in proximity to any station on the line (except Blackrock). These tickets were usually valid for three to five years, depending upon the value of the house, and the idea being that, once the tickets had expired, the owner would travel regularly on the railway. Although the railway lost revenue in the short term, the thinking behind such 'villa tickets' was sound insofar as people were encouraged to develop the land on either side of the railway – thereby ensuring a regular supply of daily commuters in the years ahead.

Ordinary fares on the CB&PR remained at roughly the same level for a number of years, the normal return fares from Cork to Crosshaven being 2s. and 1s. 6d. for first class and third class travellers respectively. On Sundays and on certain 'off-peak' periods on weekdays, the first class return was reduced to 1s. 9d., while third class returns were similarly reduced to 1s. 2d.

CB&PR Liveries

Brief details of the green livery carried by CB&PR engines during the broad gauge period were given in *Chapter One*. In practice, mid-Victorian railway companies had little choice in the matter of engine colours, green being the only viable option in terms of price and aesthetic acceptibility. Most of the 19th century companies had green engines – the only difference between the locomotives of the various railways being in the precise shade of green adopted (most of the available shades were rather drab, tending towards olive green or bottle green).

The range of paints suitable for external use at the turn-of-the-century allowed greater flexibility, the period from 1890 until 1914 being marked by a variety of diverse and attractive engine liveries. On the CB&PR, the original green colour scheme had been replaced by lined black, the lining being carried out in white and red. CB&PR coaches, meanwhile, were painted green both before and after the conversion to 3 ft gauge.

The Great Southern livery scheme was dark grey for engines and green for passenger rolling stock, though it seems that CB&PR liveries were retained for several years after the 1925 grouping.

Envoi

The remains of the Cork Blackrock & Passage line survived for many years, and traces of the route can still be discerned, Albert Street station became the offices and works of Irish Metal Products Ltd, and now of Carey Tools and other firms, and nearby Blackrock found a new lease of life as a clubhouse; it was extant in 1968, though in a derelict condition. Rochestown, in contrast, became a private dwelling and remained in good order; a dwarf box hedge was planted on the trackbed, and the island platform was retained.

Between Rochestown and Passage the formation and bridges survived intact, although Passage station had its curved (extension) platform buried in clay. The neighbouring tunnel became a useful store, oil drums being kept in the Passage end for many years.

The entrance to Passage tunnel seen in September 1968. *A.T. Newham*

A rear view of the derelict Raffeen station in September 1968. *A.T. Newham*

Elsewhere, much of the formation remained intact, and some of the masonry piers that once supported Crosshaven Viaduct could still be seen in the 1990s. Monkstown station was obliterated to make way for a car park, while at Carrigaline the former station building and goods shed were still used for storage purposes during the 1960s.

In conclusion, it may be added that the Cork Blackrock & Passage Railway suffered the fate of many other Irish railways, and in this context it is significant that most of the other Cork local lines have followed the CB&PR into ill-deserved oblivion. Many of these lines were promoted back in the 1840s when Ireland had a growing population of perhaps 9,000,000; since that time, the Irish population has steadily declined, and in an age when road transport was increasingly seen as the only solution to rural transport problems, there was no place for lightly-used narrow gauge lines such as the CB&PR.

The Cork Blackrock & Passage Railway could possibly have found a role as a tourist line, and it is interesting to speculate on just how popular it might have become if it could have survived into the 'preserved railway' era! Ironically, the nearby Cork & Youghal route from Cork to Cobh (formerly Queenstown) *has* survived, and the retention of this rival branch on the opposite side of Lough Mahon must be seen as a final twist of fate in relation to the CB&PR story.

Appendix One

Cork Blackrock & Passage Locomotives

Loco No.	Type	Date	Makers	Maker's No.	Gauge	Notes
1	2−2−2WT	1850	Sharp Bros	655	5 ft 3 in.	Withdrawn 1900
2	2−2−2WT	1850	Sharp Bros	656	5 ft 3 in.	Withdrawn 1900
3	2−2−2WT	1850	Sharp Bros	662	5 ft 3 in.	Withdrawn 1900
4	2−4−2T	1900	Neilsons	5561	3 ft	To C&L 1934[1]
5	2−4−2T	1900	Neilsons	5562	3 ft	To C&L 1934[2]
6	2−4−4T	1900	Neilsons	5563	3 ft	To C&L 1934[3]
7	2−4−2T	1900	Neilsons	5564	3 ft	To C&L 1934[4]

1. Scrapped by CIE in 1959;   2. Scrapped by GSR c.1939;   3. Scrapped by CIE in 1959;
4. Scrapped by CIE c.1950.

Appendix Two
City of Cork Proprietors Vessels

The history of the City of Cork Proprietors' fleet is complex, and further confusion arises from the way in which the company was variously referred to as 'The River Steamer Company', the 'City of Cork Proprietors' and (after 1859–60) 'The Citizen River Steamer Co. As we have seen, the CB&PR secured effective control of the fleet in 1856, but by 1860 The Citizen River Steamer Company embarked on a policy of independence which lasted until the CB&PR finally purchased the company in 1890. It follows that some vessels never passed into CB&PR control, and it would therefore be useful to list some of these non-railway steamers.

Name	Dates	GRT	Notes
PS Queen	(1838–1851?)	73 tons	Hired by CB&PR 1851
PS Maid of Erin	(c1838)	63 tons	Sold after few months service
PS Princess	(1841–56)	169 tons	
PS Pilot	(1847–51?)	79 tons	
PS Waterloo	(1816–50)	50 tons	Converted to lighter 1850
PS Kingston	(1829–80?)	106 tons	
PS City of Cork	(1815–50)	50 tons	
PS Princess Charlotte	(1821–?)		
PS Prince	(1843–61)	150 tons	
PS Prince Arthur	(1851–?)		
PS Prince of Wales	(1861–?)		
PS Lily	(1861–71)		
PS Eagle	(1838–51)	120 gross tons	engines 60 hp
PS Air	(1836–40)	70 gross tons	engines 60 hp, built River Clyde c.1825
PS Lee (I)	1830–40)	87 gross tons	engines 40 hp

Notes

City of Cork launched at Passage, 10th September, 1815 (?) First River Lee Steamer. On Cork/Cobh run until 1850. Single-masted, 86 ft long, with square stern. Engines by Boulton and Watt (12 hp), gave speed of about 6 kts. As she became older she became so decrepit that it was said a shoal of jellyfish once stopped her! In her hey-day, she carried London newspapers for patrons, and provided salt water baths.

Waterloo also locally built. Had one cylinder engine built by Hive Iron Works, Cork; probably the first marine engine built in Ireland.

Lee (I) built in London in 1825, coming to Cork in the 1830s. She too had salt water baths. Foundered off Cornish coast when returning to England 1840.

Air and Eagle said (by Dr McNeill) to have been tugs.

Appendix Three
Some Famous Personalities Associated with the CB&PR

Although the CB&PR was merely a local line, it had associations with several interesting personalities – many of them of national significance. It would, therefore, be worth concluding this brief study with short biographical notes of some of these eminent Victorians.

Sir John Macneill (1793–1880)
A graduate of Trinity College Dublin, Sir John Macneill was one of the greatest figures of the Railway Age, and he can be compared in stature with Brunel, Locke and the Stephensons. As engineer-in-chief to numerous Irish railways, he laid the foundations of the present Irish railway network; at one time this eminent engineer maintained offices in England, Ireland and Scotland! Knighted in 1844, he was Professor of Engineering at Trinity College, and wrote several engineering books. Sadly, Sir John went blind towards the end of his life, and this unfortunate affliction brought his long career to an end.

Sir John Benson (1812–1874)
Knighted for his work in connection with the Great Industrial Exhibition held in Dublin in 1853, Sir John Benson was both engineer and architect. He was, at various times, engineer to the Cork Harbour Commissioners, Cork Corporation and the County Surveyor to the East Riding of Cork; he also worked for certain GS&WR subsidiary companies, in which capacity he designed many local stations. He designed at least two relatively large stations – the CB&PR terminus at Albert Street, and the original GS&WR station at Penrose's Marsh.

William Dargan (1799–1867)
Perhaps the most famous Irishman of his day, William Dargan was a highly-successful contractor, the CB&PR being just one of his many projects. Having accepted railway shares in lieu of cash payment, Mr Dargan inevitably built up huge holdings in large numbers of Irish lines, and he eventually became Chairman of the Dublin Wicklow & Wexford Railway. His non-railway interests included sponsorship of the 1853 Dublin Exhibition, together with the promotion of new urban developments in the fashionable areas of Dublin. A casualty in the economic crisis of 1866, William Dargan died in February 1867, a riding accident having hastened his demise; in his life, he had refused knighthoods and other honours, preferring to remain 'a man of the people'.

Dr Robert Lyons (1826–1886)
An early Chairman of the CB&PR, Dr Lyons had served in the Crimean War as Chief Pathological Commissioner to the Army. In later years, he became MP for Dublin.

Acknowledgements

Thanks are due to a number of people who helped Mr Newham with his original research, among them Mr Walter McGrath (Cork) who kindly lent his albums of Irish narrow-gauge railway photos and news clippings, also other valuable data and old timetables. The Public Record Office, London provided a copy of Capt Wynne's Report and data of his inspection of the line in 1850 for the Railway Commissioners. Mr T. McSweeney, Depot Superintendent, CIE Cork, provided certain transport facilities, and Mr W. Murphy, CIE Drawing Office, Cork, after much searching, was able to produce a map of the track layout at the old City Park Station; Mr F. Cahill, Dublin prepared maps, and station layout arrangements, and Coras Iompair Eireann, Heuston Station Dublin, gave access to the Minute Books of the CB&PR.

Thanks are also due to the late Sir John Harcourt (Belfast) who furnished data from Lloyds Registry, and to the staffs of the National Library of Ireland (Dublin) who produced numerous contemporary newspapers, photographs and documents.

A general view of Monkstown station from the north.   *Irish Railway Record Society*

Further Reading

The Cork Blackrock & Passage line has enjoyed little coverage in the railway press, but several books or articles contain references to the CB&PR, and it was felt that the following brief list would be of use to those seeking further information.

H. Fayle, The Cork Blackrock & Passage Railway, *Railway Magazine* December 1909

T.L. Guest & R.D. Foster, Cork Albert Street, *Model Railway Constructor* August 1977

Patrick J. Flanagan, *The Cavan & Leitrim Railway* (1966)

Edward M. Patterson, *The County Donegal Railways*, David & Charles (1962)

David Lloyd, *Modelling the Irish Narrow Gauge*

C.L.D. Duckworth & G.E. Langmuir, *Railway & Other Steamers*, T. Stephenson & Sons (1948)

Index